unknown
What if God's not like that?

ADAM DYER

PUBLISHING

thanks

So many people have been part of this journey with me. People who have helped me form my voice, and encouraged me to use it. People who have cheered me on and supported me, and people who have contributed practically to the development of this book.

Firstly Rachel, whose love and laughter has made me the man I am today. Thanks for sharing the journey for 26 years, and for sticking with me. I think we've done a pretty good job. which brings me to our kids, Jacob, Emilia, Zac and Elijah. Thanks for being you, and hence finding your way onto the pages of this book. And thanks to all of you for giving me the space to write. To my Mum who cheered me on and verified my memories, and also my late Dad, who walked this path before me. To Mark, Nigel and Amie for their encouragement, friendship, and always being ready to listen and reflect. And thanks to Nigel and Deb Hardy who are always there, wherever they are. Our greatest friends and encouragers.

Thanks also to Yeovil Community Church for taking a chance on a dreamer and a renegade. I couldn't have made this journey without you. To the leaders for keeping me grounded and on track. To the trustees for creating the space for me to write. And to our fabulous small group for sharing life with us and bringing the fun. And to the people of YCC for your courage, generosity and faithfulness.

Thanks to all the people who have read all or part of the manuscript in its various stages and given me advice. To Nic and Steven Bastion, Jan and Malcolm Stevens, Mark Dyer, Jeremy Waite, Lydia Palfrey, Rebecca de Pelet, Joe Hardy, Cheryl Green, Dave Westlake, Steve Chalke, Brian McLaren, and Pete Greig for all the encouragement and for even attempting to find the time.

Thanks also to Robin and Bonnie Millar for crafting such a beautiful bolt hole in the mountains, and to Roger and Sue Cheale for the use of their tranquil home.

Thanks to all the others who have given me encouragement and love and moments of light through the process. You're amazing.

And thanks to God for bringing me on this crazy journey, however reluctantly I came. I'm loving it.

index

Part 3   all

Before we begin

I am a total novice at this.

I am a reluctant amateur.

I only agreed to write a book because I felt that I was supposed to do so. I didn't think I would be able to do it. I wasn't entirely sure what it would say. But I do think it says something important. There are parts of this book that stir me and excite me. There are parts of this book that are vulnerable, and some parts that have surprised me. There are experiences I didn't expect to write about, memories I didn't know I remembered, and thoughts I didn't know I had.

I am also nervous, because I release this book into a world with a lot of noise, and opinion, and anger, and defensiveness, and fear. I release this book into a global church which is divided and hurt. A church that is at odds with itself. And when fear and division and power and noise take over, we often forget how to listen.

So I want to encourage you to listen.

It is a profound truth of every person and every book and every thing, that if you want to find fault you will find it. But if you want to find Christ, you will find Him.

The question is, what are you looking for?

My intention in writing this book is not to add to the noise, or to the division. I want mine to be a voice that unifies. I want mine to be a voice that challenges people on all sides. Not a voice that shouts 'look at me', but a voice that points to Jesus. Not a voice that condemns, but a voice that invites, and draws in. And I want my words to stand or fall, not on their brilliance or foolishness, but on their love. I want them to stand or fall to the extent to which they look like Jesus. Because that's ultimately the point, right?

This is not an exercise to introduce the world to me, or to bustle my way on to the stage, it is an exercise to nudge us all towards Christ. To nudge the trajectories of the world towards justice and hope and mercy.

It's a call to unity and community.

It's an introduction, and a call to love itself.

So dive in. I really hope you enjoy it. I particularly hope that it says something to you.

Take the time to let it seep in to you, and form you.

Take the time to listen, and breathe.

And my biggest hope, is that you get to know the unknown God.

part 1

mountain

life

I became a Christian when I was eight..... I think.

I say 'I think' because it's the earliest memory I have of making a commitment, but it depends on a few things. Let me tell the story first, and then I will talk about some of the caveats.

I was eight years old, it was a Sunday evening in August, and we were about to set off on holiday. I went to a church that was led by my Dad. It was an evangelical church of around two hundred people, and it was decided that this year we would go on a church holiday to Germany. I was the youngest of three brothers and I remember being very excited. The plan was to leave shortly after the evening service, which made concentrating on the sermon difficult. And my Dad's sermons were quite long.

I remember getting to the end of the sermon and my Dad asking if anyone wanted to give their life to Jesus.

Now I'm not sure if it was a direct point of the sermon, or if it was theology I had picked up along the way, but my thought process was very clear. All these people I was with were going to heaven. My whole family. My friends. Their families. All the cool people we were going on holiday with.
Everyone.
And heaven was supposed to be great.

I was a bit mystified by how praising God for eternity could be so amazing because I struggled to last half an hour, but they all seemed really excited about it. Often to the point of tears of joy. So it must be amazing.
The problem was clearly with me.

I remember feeling really included, but I also remember that sense of inclusion being at serious risk if the end of the world should come, or something should happen. And anything could happen when you were travelling across the world.

I know it was only Europe but I was eight, give me a break.

If anything should happen, I would be going to hell and everyone else would be going to heaven.

What else was an eight year old supposed to do?

I went forward and gave my life to Jesus.

I wouldn't say much changed. I remember elation, and I'm sure that was down to God celebrating my life and giving me a huge Spirit-filled hug. But it could also have partly been because the sermon was over which meant it was time to go on our holiday. Either way, that's the moment I point to.

So, the caveats.

Firstly I had grown up in a Christian family, part of a loving church where God was evident, so I was already included and loved. To that extent maybe I have always been a Christian.

Secondly, I continued to make a number of 'decisions' at camps, events, church services, Billy Graham crusades, and times when I was on my own contemplating life. Often these were driven by a sense of having fallen short of God's standard. Times when I had broken rules, disappointed God, or drifted away. In short, guilt played a large part, differing to my first moment of conversion which was more a result of fear and self-interest.

None of which are exactly liberating or inspiring.

It's a sobering thought that even my conversion was a selfish act and so fell under the lists of sins I was being forgiven for.
A thought that troubled me at various points throughout my youth.

I remember being taught at Sunday school that the Bible stood for 'Basic Instructions Before Leaving Earth'. This book of rules and instructions was always there to tell me what to do, and more often what not to do, in order to ensure I would be included when it came to allocating spaces in heaven. I remember often feeling frustrated that I had stupidly become a Christian so young.

If I had been smarter I would have waited and done all the things I wanted to do and wasn't allowed to do, and then done a once and for all clean sweep at my conversion, ideally shortly before my death.

Hardly a life-giving gospel, more a 'get out of hell free' card that I had played too early in the game.

It was when I was twenty one that I would point to a significant change. This by no means suggests I don't consider myself a Christian until that point. God was clearly dynamically evident in my life throughout, including through some dramatically difficult times where I consider it a miracle that my faith survived at all, but that's probably for another time, or another book.

But when I was twenty one I came to the life-changing and liberating understanding that I was enough. God loved me, and Christ was in me and working through me and inviting me to go on a beautiful journey with Him. A journey of hope and love. A journey that wasn't so much about what God could do for me, but what He could do in me and through me if I let Him be God, and chose to join in His kingdom.

It was at that point I was able to see the Bible, not as a collection of rules and instructions, but as an invitation into life. An invitation into participation in the kingdom.
A life of adventure and struggle.
A life of sacrifice and vulnerability.
A life of joy and hope.
A life of beauty.

A life which I still feel a quarter of a century on has endless opportunities and unexplored aspects ahead.

Maybe that's what Jesus meant when He said He had come that we may have life in all its fullness.

different

Have you ever read a book, or heard a talk, or had a conversation, that just changed everything?

You know what I'm talking about. When something happens that changes how you look at the world, or connects with you or liberates you, or resonates with you so deeply its like you've just learnt to sing for the first time. Like you found a soul mate. Rob Bell's first book, 'Velvet Elvis' was that for me. If you haven't read it, I would encourage you to do so, once you've finished this one of course. It looks at how we have viewed the Christian faith and asks some questions.

Great questions.

The impact for me wasn't so much in hearing perspectives I hadn't heard before, but more that these were questions I'd been asking myself for a few years, I just didn't think I was allowed to ask them.

And now this book gave me permission. This book didn't just ask the questions, it shouted them from the rooftops with a hope and a freedom that had been missing for me. It called out something from inside of me that I had been trying to verbalise for years.

It was like finding the words for a favourite symphony.
I had known the tune for a while, but now I had the words,
I could sing along.

At the time Rob Bell led a church called Mars Hill in Grand Rapids where he was working out some of these questions and ideas to see what God looked like and what church could be like. I would listen to the podcast from time to time, and would often hear him talking about ideas and questions I was wrestling with at the same time. It felt like we were on a similar journey.

On one of my searches, I discovered another church called Mars Hill, in Seattle. One of my favourite cities. I assumed it was a sister church and downloaded a couple of the podcasts.

It wasn't quite the same.

This church was led by a guy called Mark Driscoll. Not as hipster as Rob Bell but a very good communicator, just like Rob. He was funny, dynamic, and clearly loved scripture too. And he was just as effective at drawing in the crowds. Both churches were huge and cool, and culturally relevant. Both had a large international following and saw thousands impacted and declaring their faith in Jesus.

And yet what they were preaching was quite different.
The tone was different.
The heart was different.
The theology was different.

Both Christian churches.
Both worshipping God.
Both encouraging faith in Jesus. and yet they couldn't be more different.

Same scriptures and yet very different out-workings of those same scriptures.

Same God, and yet very different ideas of what that God is like.

Which leads us to some very big questions.

Can they both be right?

How should we read the Bible?

And what is God like?

unknown

It might surprise some to know that Mars Hill isn't just the name of a couple of very different churches in America. It is also a place in its own right. It's a fairly simple place. A bit rocky. A bit grassy. Just space really. In many ways quite nondescript except for its views over Athens below and the Acropolis above.

But it's a significant place. Because this is where the council of elders of Athens would gather. It's where the men would sit and discuss life, the meaning of life and the role of the gods. It is where they would pass judgement on criminals. It is the site in mythology where the gods would sit in judgement too. And it's the site where Paul addressed the men of Athens and talked about their monument to the unknown god.

On the walk up the hill from the Agora To the Acropolis, the path was lined by statues to the gods. All the usual suspects were there along with all sorts of other, less famous gods. It was important to the Greeks to have their bases covered when it came to recognising and honouring the gods, and so all sorts of gods were there, including a monument to the unknown god.

Probably in case they had missed one.

Because when your life, and welfare, and city, and civilisation is dependent on keeping the gods on side, then you find yourself covering a lot of bases and walking on a lot of eggshells.

So in Acts 17 we see this story where Paul is brought before the council on Mars Hill to explain the gospel he has been preaching about Jesus, and he cites this altar with the inscription

'to the unknown god'

and challenges them that they worship what they don't know.

Worship a god they don't even know?

Like any of us would do something like that.

A few years ago, I visited Athens with my wife and some friends and we walked up to the Acropolis, passing the sites of statues and altars all the way up. On our way up we spent some time on Mars Hill. We looked at the views over Athens, watched people flying kites, and stood where Paul had stood on that day and imagined what it was like to walk into this culture which was highly religious, and talk about a new god. An unknown god.

Can you imagine what it must have been like worshipping a god you don't even know? Worried that you might have offended this faceless god, or feeling like you aren't good enough for him in some way. Or afraid that he wants to punish you for something, or that the bad harvest you just had, or the sickness in your family, or the war you just lost, or the exam you just failed, happened because this unknown god was unhappy about something.

Sounds horrible, doesn't it?

And so you would make sacrifices and offerings to this god in the hope that he would change his mind and bless you instead. You would pray to this god, and all the other gods, so that they would stop the rain, or heal your child, or change your fortunes, or make you win the war. And these sacrifices or offerings could include all sorts of things. Things like money, jewellery, clothes, food or even children. All in the hope that this god would stop being angry and bring an end to the punishment.

We ended up sharing this visit to Mars Hill and the Acropolis with a large party of Americans. They were all on a cruise following the missionary journeys of Paul and it just so happened that our visit to Athens coincided with theirs. There were hundreds, maybe thousands, of them swarming over Mars Hill and filling the walk up to the Acropolis and the Parthenon. It added a certain buzz to the occasion.

When we reached the Acropolis I sat on a large chunk of marble and gazed at the Parthenon. If you haven't seen it, you must go. It is stunning. This centre of pantheism. Where mythology is told all around you. This place where the gods and the people come together and share space. It really is stunningly beautiful and awe inspiring. The design of the temples is so clever and intricate. They work on measured imperfection to create an illusion of perfection. The columns slightly bulge in the middle so when the sunlight shines through they appear straight. The steps have a camber to them which makes them appear level from a distance. The dimensions of the temples are all just off so that they appear balanced. And then there's the sculptures and statues. They are so beautifully and painstakingly carved.

Breathtaking.

As I took in the beauty, I noticed I was no longer alone on my hunk of marble. Two ladies from the cruise party had joined me and I couldn't resist engaging them in conversation. They explained they were on this cruise to learn more about Paul's missionary journeys and so they visited a number of sites during the cruise. These included Corinth, Athens, Rome, Ephesus and Venice.

Venice? I must have missed that chapter.

We joked about how many shipwrecks were on the schedule so they could get a real feel for Paul's journeys and experiences, and we discussed how the cruise had brought the Bible to life for them. It was a lot of fun. And then I asked them, as a result of their trip and immersion in the story of Paul, what did they understand was Paul's primary message in his letters?

They ooh'ed and ahh'ed and then said, 'Gee, I guess it was that we should all get on. You know, like when there is a choir master and a choir that don't see eye to eye, they shouldn't be mean to each other, but choose to be friends and work together'.

The conversation seemed to come to an end then, not least because I didn't know quite what to say. Paul's main message was that choirs and choirmasters should bury the hatchet? I had long since had questions around how people read the Bible and used Paul's letters, but interestingly this caused me to think about what Paul's principle message really was,

Because I wasn't sure that it was about choirs and choirmasters.

As I read through Paul's letters, the theme that came to the fore, over and over, was the theme of grace over law. Time and time again he declares us children of grace, recipients of grace, free from the law, and delivered from the law. He urges us not to put ourselves back under law again but to live in the freedom we have been given. He declares that the law could not save us, but that the death and resurrection of Jesus Christ has saved us and liberated us.

Time and time again.

Grace over law.

Not under law.

A gospel of grace.

And pleading with us to not continue to live under the law.

Which all raises a very good question.

If Paul's principle message was grace over law, why have we used his writings to construct a whole new law?

Paul's law is so prevalent in our churches.

Whether women are allowed to lead or speak. How we should dress. How we treat or use our bodies. Tattoos, piercings, sex, sexual orientation, giving, who can take communion, how we take communion.

The list just goes on and on and on.

But if Paul's principle message was grace, have we got it wrong?

If Paul urged us not to return to legalistic ways, then have we spectacularly missed the point?

Is Paul currently in a soundproof room in heaven screaming and shouting at just what we have done with his letters?

And why did Paul think the law was such a problem?

storehouses

Towards the end of Genesis, we see the story of Joseph.

Joseph is the eleventh of twelve brothers who are all sons of Jacob, who is son of Isaac, who is son of Abraham. This is the family who God has said He will make into a nation, and they will be a blessing to all the other nations. They will outnumber the stars in the sky and they will make God known to the world and through them the world will know what God is like.

That's quite a responsibility for a family.

Joseph finds himself in prison in Egypt, having been sold by his brothers. He is in exile, a prisoner and a follower of the God of Abraham, Isaac and Jacob. And it's fair to say that things don't appear to be going to plan.

One night Pharaoh has a dream which troubles him. A dream of seven healthy, plump cows which are eaten by seven scrawny cows, and the dream scares him. So he calls all his mystics and wise men together, and asks them to interpret it.

A task they find impossible.

But Joseph is good at dreams and Pharaoh gets to hear about this, and so Pharaoh calls him. Pharaoh recounts his dream, and Joseph explains the meaning to him. There will be seven years of plenty followed by seven years of famine, and the dream is a warning from God and an instruction to store food over the seven good years, so that no one from Egypt or the surrounding nations goes without during the years of famine.

An act of good stewardship.
An act of compassion and generosity.
An act of care and love for the people.

Pharaoh asks Joseph to be the man who takes control of this programme and make sure that everyone has what they need. It is during this famine that Joseph's brothers travel to Egypt to plead for food because they are starving. The famine has left them desperate. And so they go to Egypt and come face to face with their long lost brother who they thought was dead.

Joseph is reunited with his family. As a result of this encounter, Joseph's family and all the tribes of Israel move to live in Egypt. It's a beautiful story of redemption and restoration. A story of hope. A story that shows us that God is a God who calls us towards unity and life. A God who is about forgiveness and wholeness. A God of grace. And, coming at the end of Genesis, it gives us a hint of the sort of trajectory God is calling us on. An idea of the sort of trajectory we are going to see through scripture. One that arcs towards hope and restoration. One that arcs towards justice and inclusion of the other. One that arcs towards love.

But it's a story that quickly seems to go wrong. Even before we get to the end of Genesis, we are told that this act of generosity has started to become oppressive. This project of justice has become unjust. When people have run out of money, they approach Joseph, still starving and desperate for food. Joseph takes their cattle as payment. When their cattle are all gone he takes their land, and when their land is all gone he takes them as slaves.

Four hundred years on and we are at the beginning of Exodus. The Israelites are now a huge tribe of people, and Egypt has become fearful of them and made them all slaves.

Because that's what we do when we are fearful and threatened. We oppress and dehumanise the other.
We harden and diminish our own hearts.

But what is it that Egypt is forcing this vast tribe of slaves to build?

Storehouses.

And not just storehouses.

Whole cities just to store food.

The Israelite slaves are building storehouses for Egypt so they can store more and more food. This is the same act that God had instructed four hundred years earlier as an act of compassion, kindness, generosity and love. But now that same act is motivated by greed and fear. It has become destructive and oppressive rather than life-giving and liberating.

The same act with a different heart.

Same action.
Different heart.

How often do we see that?

Something that God has given us, or shown us, or called us to do. Something that started out as being beautiful and invigorating and a blessing, can move from being life-giving and redemptive to being destructive and life-sapping and full of death.

It goes from being liberating to being oppressive.
It goes from being something that brings joy to being something that brings hurt and pain and division.

It becomes all about power.

Same action.
Different heart.

And we keep going, insisting that God is in it and it's God's will or God's way even though it stopped looking like God a long time ago.

We keep going despite people getting damaged, or hurt or even leaving, because its clearly what God instructed us to do and so anyone who disagrees is obviously wrong and anti-God.

And the more people oppose it, the stronger and more insistent we get. The more legalistic and fundamental we get.

And we end up using the people we were meant to save to build our empire and make us bigger and bigger storehouses for more and more of our wealth.

Or bigger and bigger churches for more and more of our fame, or success, or people or whatever we measure.

And it stopped looking like God a long time ago.

And our hearts get smaller and harder.
And our world gets more restrictive and oppressive.
And power and control and greed get deep into us.
Until God has to intervene,

and save His people

from

us.

like

Egypt was a nation that believed in a lot of gods. Its strength and its life source came from the river Nile and so there was a god of the river. There was a god of the harvest. A god of the weather. A god of the skies. A god of the earth. A god of the sun. A god of the cattle. A god of the afterlife. A god of fertility. A god of the newborn. A god of love. A god of justice. A god of marriage, and a god of baboons.

gods for everything.

Even Pharaoh himself was declared a son of the gods, and a visible representation of god on earth.

Which we might come back to.

And all these gods were temperamental and demanding. If you upset them in some way then the river would stop providing food, the sun would scorch the crops, the rain would flood the city, the cattle would get sick, the children would be stillborn, the wars would be lost....

You get the idea.

Which meant that the Egyptians spent a lot of time trying to keep these gods happy. They had an intricate sacrifice and offering system to appease the gods. They had temples and priests and rules to help the people manage the gods. And there was a belief that if you were able to know the true name of a god, then you would have power over it.

So when God appears to Moses and tells him to go to Pharaoh, the son of the gods, and tell him to let the Israelites go, Moses wants a name so he can say who sent him. Because if you are going to go face to face with a god and tell him something he doesn't want to hear, you need some cards in your hand, and the name of a more powerful god is a useful card to play. And to suggest that you have some control over this god, or that this god is on your side, is a really good card to play. And everyone wants to know the name of God and have Him on their side, and so Moses asks God for His name to which He replies

I AM WHO I AM

Which doesn't really help Moses, because God is saying that this isn't about power and control, and He isn't just another god for Moses to know about and have influence over,

He is God.

This is a whole other kind of relationship.

God has heard the cry of His people, and He wants to free them and establish them as a nation who are a light for the world, and He will be with them, and for them, and He will be known by them and through them.

So when God saves the Israelites from Egypt, and brings them through the Red Sea, God doesn't just save them geographically, He needs to save them spiritually and socially too.

It is one thing to get them out of Egypt, but He also needs to get Egypt out of them.

Because Egypt has become rooted in them.

The culture of not enough.
The culture of power and oppression.
The culture of fear.
The culture of us against them.
The dehumanisation.
The gods that they have learned to serve and depend on.
The culture that says that gods should be manipulated and appeased.

They need to be saved from all of it.

God doesn't just save them geographically,
He needs to save them spiritually and socially too.

It is one thing to get them out of Egypt,
He also needs to get Egypt out of them.

Because Egypt has become rooted in them.

And so as God calls them out. He reminds them again and again who they are and who He is.

He reminds them again and again that He is not like those gods of Egypt. He is not temperamental, angry or petty. He does not need to be appeased or manipulated. He does not oppress or dehumanise. He is not vindictive or insecure.

He reminds them that He is the God of Abraham, Isaac and Jacob. The God of their forefathers.
The God who has journeyed with them,
The God who does not forget them.
The God who hears their cry.
The God who has made promises to them that he wants to fulfil.
The God of covenant.

He reminds them that they are His people, who He has called to show the world what He is like. Not just for their own benefit, but so that they can be a blessing to the nations.
He tells them that they are to be a visible representation of the invisible God. And that how they live is to be a light to the tribes and nations around them. A declaration of the nature of God.

And so he gives them the law.

Not to constrain them or crush them, because God's not like that, but to liberate them from who they had become and the culture they had been subject to.

A law to liberate them from their oppressed mindset of not having enough and not being enough.
A law to remind them of their God-given identity and to see them become a light and a blessing to all nations.
A law to prepare them for the land He had prepared for them.
A land to bless them.
A place where He could be with them.
A place of peace and blessing and community and love.

Because that's what God is like.

enough

Last year we were on holiday with friends in Croatia. We decided to hire a boat and ride along the coast. We had a fabulous time, except for a couple of precarious moments which aren't for now. Towards the end of this boat ride, we went into a harbour to have a look around. It was a really pretty little place with a lot of life going on. The harbour was full of all sorts of boats and yachts.

In one area of the harbour we saw a really beautiful yacht. It was stunning. Sleek lines, blacked out windows and jet skis sat on the back. It must have cost a fortune. A really amazing yacht. The problem was that it was docked between two huge yachts, with even sleeker lines, and even more windows and decks, and one of them had jet skis and a speed boat sat on the back, and the other had what I think was a mini submarine.

The owner of the first yacht probably thought he had really made it. He probably thought he had arrived at the top of the pile, the richest guy in town. And then not one bigger yacht rocked up, but two. And not just a little bit bigger. A lot bigger, which presents the owner of the first yacht with a choice.

Does he look up or does he look down?

If he looks up, he risks feeling poor. Stood on a sleek beautiful yacht that costs millions, but still feeling poor, because the other guy has more.

If he looks down, he sees me, in a rental boat that barely goes. By no means poor, after all I am on a holiday in Croatia and having a lovely time with great friends, but certainly not in the same financial position as him.

The problem is that the world teaches us to look up rather than down. The world drives it in to us that we need more.

We are all 25% away from enough.

A study was done in America recently where people who earned $250,000 a year were asked if they considered themselves to be high income earners.

30% of them did not consider themselves to be.

Another study was done asking a group of millionaires if they thought they were rich.

40% did not think that they were rich.

I'll leave that with you for a minute.

Another study was done asking multimillionaires, which in this case meant people who had wealth ranging from $25m to $2bn, if they felt financially secure.

$2,000,000,000

Over 50% said that they did not feel financially secure.

More than half.....

A follow-up question was asked of the people who felt that they weren't financially secure. They were asked how much more they would need to feel financially secure. And this is the amazing bit. Across the board they suggested that they would need around 25% more.

Whether they had $25million or $2billion they needed 25% more.

Which leads us to a couple of conclusions.

Firstly, it seems that the more we have, the poorer we feel.

The statistics go from 30% to 40% to over 50% as the amounts get bigger. It's almost like the system traps us into a dependency. It ties us into a system that is always driving us to have more, and as we play along and acquire more, so our need grows. And it consumes us, and distorts us. However much wealth we might have, we believe that if we could just get that bit more then we would be content; until we achieve that pay rise, or that holiday, or that new car, or that bigger house, and then we realise that we are still wanting more.

Still not enough. Still 25% away.

Maybe this is why Jesus said it is harder for a rich man to get into the kingdom of heaven than it is for a camel to get through the eye of a needle. Because when we are trapped in this system of not enough, we become distorted and discontent and we find it impossible to extricate ourselves from this mindset that says we are not enough, and that we need more.

Which is probably why prosperity teaching is so popular. Because it tells us that God agrees with us. We need more. And so God becomes an investment plan rather than a life plan.

Secondly, these statistics tell us that enough is not an amount. 'Enough' is an attitude.
A perspective.
A choice.
If we have $25m then we need $6m more to have enough, but when we get there, we feel like we are $8m away. All the way up to having $2bn and only being $500m away.
Enough is a perspective, and an attitude, and so it is a choice. Enough is right here right now if we choose it. But never here, and never now if we listen to the messages all around us. Because we live in and celebrate a culture of not enough.

When the Israelites were in slavery, they lived in a culture of not enough. They didn't have enough freedom, enough food, enough time, and they didn't have enough straw to make the bricks with. Pharaoh was always demanding more from them.
And they were slaves in a nation that was always building more storehouses. Because they were afraid of not having enough. This was a cultural problem. A societal problem. A circumstantial problem.

Imagine that. A major empire with huge resources and power, and yet the culture is one of always needing more. A culture of lack. A culture of never having enough.

This was their story.

And 'not enough' was a culture God needed to save them from. Because it gets into our soul. It stops us living expansive and generous lives. It distorts how we see the world. It shrinks us and hardens us and makes us mean.

And so God told them to give.

He told them to give 10% of what they had, because it liberates us from the mentality of not enough. It teaches us generosity which in turn expands our hearts and restores our humanity, and our ability to contribute and love.

But in addition God also told them to give their first fruits. This meant that at the beginning of the harvest, before anything else, their first instinct should be one of giving away. To teach them the instinct of giving, God told them that their first response to receiving anything, should be to give away. That they should be instinctively generous.

But God didn't leave it there. In addition to a habit of generosity, and an instinct of generosity, God also told them to consider the poor. And this is the brilliant bit. Because God says don't keep looking at those that have more than you. Don't keep looking at those who have bigger yachts, because that teaches you an attitude of not enough, and it makes you mean and shrinks your heart. Instead focus on the people who have less, the guys in the little rental boat, and be generous to them. Share what you have with them. Because this will teach you gratitude. It will expand your hearts and remind you how to love. It will teach you justice and compassion and restore your humanity.

God didn't tell the Israelites to give because He needed the money. He didn't tell them to give to prove how committed they were. He didn't tell them to give so they could appease Him.

It wasn't a condition of their salvation.
But it was a path of salvation.

It was a habit that would save them from who they had become.
It would save them from the society they had grown up in.
It would extricate them from the mindset they had learnt.

It was part of their exodus.

Giving is such a contentious subject in the church today. I see so many people giving out of expectation. People giving to appease, to assure their place in heaven. I see people giving as part of an investment plan, with the expectation that God will give them more back. I see people giving out of fear, people giving out of greed, people giving out of expectation.

Same action.
Different heart.

Something God invites us to do as part of our liberation. Something that will save us from the mindset of not enough. Something that will teach us to look at the world, and ourselves, and others differently, becomes legalistic, oppressive, joyless, life-sapping and guilt-ridden.

Same action.
Different heart.

God invites us to give. To be generous. To live expansively. To see the blessing flow through us into the world around us. God invites us to have the attitude of enough. To recognise that we have enough, and that we are enough.

God says you are enough.

tithe

By the time we get to the New Testament, the laws about giving are essentially the same, but the outworking of them is quite different.

They still give 10% of what they have. They still give first fruits, and they at least make the gesture of considering the poor, but we see a quite different outworking of that law.

We don't see a law that is there to liberate or to transform. We don't see a law that is teaching contentment and providing enough for everyone. And we don't see a law that is teaching people to look at the world differently, expansively or generously.

We see a law that is perpetuating the divide between rich and poor. We see a law that is excluding people. We see a law that burdens and oppresses people. We see a law that plays on expectation, guilt and fear, rather than freedom, joy and love.

They are still giving, tithing and offering, but it is the same action with a different heart.

And this is what Jesus picks up on when he challenges the religious leaders of Israel.

> 'Woe to you, teachers of the law and Pharisees, you hypocrites! You give a tenth of your spices - mint, dill and cumin. But you have neglected the more important matters of the law - justice, mercy and faithfulness. You should have practiced the latter without neglecting the former. You blind guides! You strain out a gnat but swallow a camel.'
>
> NIV

It's hard to see why He was so unpopular with the religious leaders.

The law said that to consume any living or unclean animal was a sin that would render you unacceptable to God. So Jesus picks up on their habit of straining out gnats from their drinks in order to avoid consuming an unclean or living animal. The religious and devout people would put mesh over their drinks to stop bugs getting in because they didn't want to break the law. It's a bit like how people put a wedge of lime in the mouth of a Mexican beer bottle. It's not just a flavour thing, it's a hygiene thing. It was often done to stop flies getting into the beer.

Jesus highlights this practice as an extreme measure to go to in order to keep the law. But He then charges them with consuming a camel, which is a ridiculous image. The concept of a camel in your drink is an image that is meant to be shocking. A camel was one of the biggest unclean animals in the Jewish faith. So Jesus is pointing out that whilst they take great care in their attention to detail over the law by straining out the smallest animal or bug, they miss the fact that there is a huge camel in their drink. This is a powerful and effective allegory to the crowd listening. The charge He lays at their feet is that they are paying extreme attention to the letter of the law, but at the same time completely missing the overarching theme of the law: the guiding principles of justice, mercy and faithfulness.

They are following the law to the letter and at the same time entirely missing the point.

Jesus stresses to them that the law only makes sense when you apply it in the context of the heart of the law, which is justice, mercy and faithfulness. When you see it as a law that is there to liberate, include, transform, and reveal the nature of God, then it makes sense, but when you see it as a list of rules to be kept, it becomes oppressive, overbearing and exclusive, painting God as distant, angry, mean, unjust, unloving, vindictive and inaccessible. Jesus calls them hypocrites for presenting an image of being holy and like God, when in fact they are living in total opposition to the nature and character of God.

Something we will pick up further in a while.

millionaire

We all want to know how to do something. Whether its how to play a particular tune on the piano, or how to get rich quick, how to lose weight, how to be successful, how to be beautiful, or how to make friends and influence people. Or we want to know how to get that girl to notice me, or date me, or sleep with me or marry me. We're all looking for the magic key, the secret, the abc, the seven steps.

We're all looking for the formula.

And the Christian world is no different. We want to know how to heal people, how to hear God well, how to get to heaven, how to be a worship leader or preacher, how to plant a church, how to grow a church, how to know our calling, how to fulfil our calling, how to speak in tongues, how to get more spiritual gifts, how to be blessed and how to get rich.

Hardly counter-cultural.

A little while ago I was in Brazil and heard a story of a conference of pastors in Sao Paulo where the speaker said that God had told him that He wanted to make people millionaires that day. He said anyone who wanted to be a millionaire should come forward and give him $10,000 as a sign of their faith, and God would make them a millionaire.

Over 100 pastors responded.

Which meant that at least one person was made a millionaire that day, but I would suggest it had little to do with God.

These pastors were all looking for the formula. If I put in $10,000 then God would give me $1,000,000. It seems crazy that they should fall for it, except that many pastors preach the same thing. If you put so much in the offering, God will give you 10 times that back. We turn giving into the greatest investment plan in history.

We sell a formula rather than a relationship.

And we don't just do it with money.

formula

I don't know if you've ever read 'The Rainbow' by D H Lawrence but it was one of my 'A' Level texts and I hated it. I don't know how much was to do with the plot, which is somewhat repetitive, or my particular teacher, who was somewhat dull, but I could not get into the book at all.
I'm sure you can all relate.

My other teacher, who taught my other text,was brilliant. If you've seen Robin Williams' performance in Dead Poets Society then you might have an idea of the madness and brilliance of Mr Shewan.

Mr Shewan taught me 'The Power and The Glory' by Graham Greene. It remains one of my most loved novels.

The Power and The Glory is a beautiful, pained novel of the last priest in a South American police state. He is a wreck of a priest, with addictions and hang-ups and an illegitimate child, all of which play into his long story of shame and failure. He is convinced that God has given up on him. God is disappointed in him. And so he gives up on God, and goes on the run. The beautiful thing is that whilst he is on the run he is able to bring hope and redemption in a hopeless situation. Despite his best efforts not to. As the story progresses he comes face to face with his failure and shame. He sees the failed and pathetic priest he is trying to run away from, and yet, as he loses more and more of his religious trappings, he discovers more and more of God and of hope. It is a beautiful story of the restrictions of religion and the pain of failure, but also the beauty and hope of God despite all of this.
A simply stunning novel.

I do not hold similar love for 'the Rainbow'. I found it impossible to access, and so I would often drift off in lessons and contemplate life. It was during one of these monotonous, seemingly interminable lessons that I started writing some thoughts on a pad I had in front of me. I do not remember anything of the lesson, but I do remember writing a phrase about religion that has stuck with me ever since.

All religion is man made, and packages God into something we can use to control and manipulate people.

I don't know where it came from. Maybe it was inspired by Graham Greene, or maybe it was a result of what I had experienced, but I instinctively knew that this wasn't restricted to my experience. This was a universal issue.

Which is a strange thing for a church leader to say.

So often we see God defined, or used, to support someone's point of view, or calling, or theology, or political opinion, or prejudice, or anger or behaviour. We see God used to justify wars, or hate crimes, or discrimination, or violence, or wealth, or greed, and the list goes on. And then we see Him used to convince others to join in with this behaviour.

We see God treated like a genie who will grant wishes or make people rich, or like Santa Claus who will bless all the good people and decide who's been naughty or nice. Except the people who define God this way, also do so in a way that never has them allocated to the naughty list.

It isn't too different from what the Egyptians believed.

The Egyptians believed that if you knew the true name of a god you gained an element of power over him or her. If you knew the name or character of a god, then you had a level of connection with that god that meant you could harness that god's power to serve your purposes. That god would be on your side now. Fight your battles now. Give you blessings and victories and power. And whilst we use different language in the 21st century and we like to think that our religion is a little more sophisticated and nuanced, it remains true that we have power over a god we get to define. And if we follow that to its natural conclusion, we get situations where people set themselves up as the mouthpiece of their god and use it to preserve privilege, protect position, control people, exclude, dehumanise, diminish and oppress.

And so we put a lot of energy into setting up systems of belief, rules of behaviour, and rituals of sacrifice and worship.

And they can be quite elaborate,

because it all helps me package God.

If I know what to believe, and the rules I am supposed to live by, then I don't need God anymore. If I have the formula, then I know what I need to know and what I need to do to make sure I get into heaven and get God on my side. If God is on my side then He will give me blessings, victories, and power. He will answer my prayers, protect me from harm, set out my paths, and make sure I prosper and have enough.

But there's a problem with this.

If I can know the rules, rituals and beliefs that I have to follow to keep my side of the bargain, then it puts me back in control.

I can control myself to meet all the requirements and so put God in a position where He is compelled to accept me and bless me and save me. He has to keep his side of the bargain.

If I say the right prayer, follow all the right rules, believe all the right things and observe the right rituals, then God is contractually obliged to accept me, because that's the deal.

But that doesn't sound much like a god at all.

Because we are the ones with all the power.

It is a worthwhile thought that if our god only ever validates us and affirms us as being right, and everyone else being wrong, then maybe our god looks a little bit too much like us. Which could suggest that maybe we have created god in our image rather than allowing God to create us in His image.

But what if God is bigger than that?

We make God so small, and convenient. We talk about a God who fits in the neatly drawn lines of our world-view. But God is so much bigger than that. If I can define God, or name God, then it isn't God, because if God is God, then he has to be bigger than I can imagine or conceive of. It has to be possible that other understandings and experiences of God exist that don't fit within my own understanding, which calls to mind something one of my Bible college lecturers said.

Don't be surprised when God continues to save people by ways you cannot approve of.

Deal with it.

He's God.

You're not.

This is something that the Israelites seemed to grasp.

In a world where every nation had their own gods that reflected their national identity, the writers of Genesis seemed to get this idea that God is bigger than that.

Genesis was written while the Israelites were in exile in Babylon. It was, and still is, a Jewish tradition to pass on stories to the next generation and the next. And so when the Israelites were in exile in Babylon, living in oppression and slavery

again

they told stories that had been passed down by their ancestors. They told tales of how God had formed the world, brought the flood, called out Abraham to father a nation, and brought that nation to its own land, the promised land, as a people who would show the world something of what God was like. And during that exile they decided to write some of these stories down, to retain their identity. And this is important to understand, because they were in another culture, who worshipped their own gods, who were quite different to Jehovah, the God of Israel and the world. And Babylon had their own creation story, and their own flood story, which were quite different.

The Babylonian creation story paints a picture of creation being formed as a result of conflict between two gods. After one god destroyed the other, he tore the carcass in two, using half to form the earth and the other half to form the skies. Creation came as a result of death, violence, and destruction.

The Hebrew creation story we find in Genesis tells a very different story. It tells a story of God being in interdependent relationship with Himself as Father, Son and Spirit. In this story we see God speaking creation into being, bringing forth life and beauty. We see God speaking the universe into reality. A God who creates space, and then fills it with vibrant life. And then God invites us to join in. God invites us to be in relationship with Him and to continue the process of creation, and life, and vibrancy.

Genesis goes on to tell how God called Abraham to leave his homeland of power and might, leaving behind all the comfort and privilege that came with that, and set off on a journey somewhere else where God would lead. And God promised that He would raise

Abraham up as father of a nation, and that God would love and lead that nation. But God made it clear that He wouldn't just bless that nation, but instead that He would bless the whole earth through that nation.

A God who wasn't just there *for* the people who worship Him, or there just to *bless and save* the people who worship Him, but a God who wanted to bless and save the whole world *through* the people who worship Him.

Because God is bigger than that, and he invites us to be bigger too.

What if we could allow God to break free from the boxes and systems we have used to confine Him?
What if we could let go of our need for certainty, and instead embrace the questions, and doubts, and wonder of God?
What if we could see God through other people's experiences which are different to our own?
What if we could work in partnership with God to see all nations and all people blessed?

And what if, like the priest in the Power and the Glory, we were able to lose our religious trappings, and break free from the religious mindset that says we aren't good enough, and find God in the middle of our mess?

What if we could break free from the formula and the fear?

What if we chose to not be in control, but instead we could find the courage to submit, and step into a relationship with this God?

Would we find a God who looked completely different to the God we expected?

Would we find out that God isn't like that?

mountain

After God saves the Israelites from their slavery and oppression in Egypt, it is evident that there is more work to be done. God has saved them geographically but, as we have seen, He needs to save them socially and spiritually too. This is why God gives them the law. Not just the Ten Commandments, but all the social laws too. All the laws of sacrifice, hygiene, community, behaviour, ritual and rhythm. God is not trying to just put a new set of demands on them so they can appease Him and prevent Him from destroying them or punishing them,

God is always trying to liberate them. Always.

God is always trying to see them fulfil their God-given identity.

God is always calling them forwards into more.
More humanity.
More community.
More relationship with Him.
More wholeness.
More hope.
More forgiveness.
More truth.
More.

And so, as a community they need laws.
They need structure.
They need rhythm.

And so, after God has liberated them from slavery and brought them out into the wilderness, God takes time to stop and begin the work of building community and identity. The work of liberation has to continue, from the geographical to the spiritual and social. And so God calls Moses up the mountain so He can equip him and give him the law. But this is where it gets interesting. Moses has to go up the mountain into the presence of God, but the Israelites need to stay at the bottom. Indeed at one point they plead with Moses to go up and meet with God, and get the law, and to tell them the rules. The people promise to obey them, doing whatever God says, but they also plead with Moses to not make them go up, or even set foot on the mountain, because they would die.

So God is at the top of the mountain, and the people are at the bottom, in fear of their lives. Terrified that God will kill them.
Because that's what religion and legalism does.
It tells us that God is angry with us and we need to appease Him.
It tells us that only the very best will make it.
It sets the bar high.

And religion and legalism keep us rooted at the bottom of the mountain.

Distant but drawn.
Ashamed but enthralled.
Afraid but desperate.

It tells us over and over again, that God is angry, and that we aren't good enough, but that we need Him and can't live without Him. And so, it maintains the divide between us and God. It keeps us rooted at the bottom and God distant at the top. It keeps us afraid rather than loved. It keeps telling us that if we see God, we will die.

And so, we crave the formula. Tell us what to believe. Tell us what to do. But don't make us look at God in the face, because we will die. Don't make me go up the mountain.

So we need the priests and prophets who will tell us what God says with amazing confidence. We need the leaders and the preachers to tell us what to believe and what to do. We need the books about Jesus, and the Bible studies, and the statements of belief, and the theological expositions and the memory verses.

Remember those?

We need the clever biblical answers to difficult questions, and the pastors who speak in absolutes, but please don't make me hear God for myself. Please don't make me wrestle with scripture myself. Please don't make me encounter God for myself. Face to face. Please don't make me go up the mountain, because I just might die.

There is something in us that so often wants to avoid God. Even when we have had amazing moments and encounters. We are happy to sing about Him, talk about Him, even tell others about Him. But to actually stop, let everything fall away and look Him in the face. That is terrifying.
And so we tell stories about Him. Stories that we have heard.
We tell people the theological truths about Him and call it evangelism.
We sing theological truths about Him and call it worship.
And we study what the Bible says about Him and call it discipleship.

Now please don't misunderstand me. None of these things are wrong in themselves. They all have their place. But the point of worship, and prayer, and discipleship, and evangelism is relationship. The point of them all is Jesus. God revealed and known. The point of them all is a beautiful and terrifying abandonment into complete relationship with God. The God of the universe encountering me in the most beautiful and powerful way, and liberating me.

And it doesn't stop with me. We do this together. So we encounter God together, with each other, through each other, for each other, and for 'the other'. For the outcast, the exile and the enemy.

And what we see time and time again is that religiosity and legalism stop us doing exactly that. The Law keeps us rooted at the foot of the mountain, desperate for someone to tell us what God says, or what to do, or what to believe. And it leaves us convinced that we aren't good enough, and we aren't enough for this God.

A God who is angry and distant.
A God who is separate, and needs to be protected.
A God who has been silent for so long.
A God who speaks to the special people, but not to us.
A God who wants to punish and destroy us if we fail.
A God who afflicts us, and causes our suffering.
A God who whimsically decides who lives and who dies.
A God who we fear but don't love.
A God who suffers us, and demands from us, but doesn't love us.
A God who we know about,

but a God we don't know.

An unknown god.

irrelevant

This is the world Paul had been living in.
The world of formula.
The world of not enough.
The world where God must be feared, appeased, and kept apart.
The world of distance.
The world of packaging God into something we can use to control
and manipulate.
The world of power and privilege.
The world of exclusivity and religiosity.

We meet Paul in the book of Acts, in the New Testament. Acts tells
the story of what happens after the resurrection of Jesus. It tells
the story of how the disciples took the story of Jesus into the
Jewish world and then beyond, into the rest of the world. And Paul
was instrumental in this. Paul was a part of the Jewish religious
system which Jesus had come to overthrow, and so Paul was an
enemy of Jesus, and the followers of Jesus. He was hunting down
followers of Jesus to try them, and kill them.

Paul had ended up persecuting the very God he was worshipping.
His passion for the law had resulted in him failing to recognise God
when He was right in front of him.

And Paul wasn't just a follower of this law, Paul was an expert in
the law. Paul was an enforcer of the law. He was a fanatic, chasing
down anyone who stepped outside the law. Hunting down followers
of Jesus because they threatened the religious system, and the
religious leaders, and power brokers of Israel. Paul was a defender
of the law. He was zealous in his pursuit of holiness. Passionate in
his desire to follow God, and see Israel restored to its glory as the
nation of God.

And yet it's Paul who says elsewhere in the Bible that 'we are free
from the law' and 'don't let anyone put you under the law', and
even 'the law is irrelevant'. He calls the law a curse, and insists
that the law can save nobody.

So what happened?

In Philippians Paul talks about his obsession with the law and how it had left him bereft. He makes the bold claim that he kept the law perfectly. If the law was the way, then he had cracked it. But in fact his zealous adherence to the law, in all its detail, was now as nothing to him. It hadn't succeeded in bringing him closer to God, it had taken him in the other direction. It hadn't saved him, it had entrapped him. It hadn't made him holy, but instead had left him proud and powerful, oppressing and killing those who followed Jesus. The Messiah himself.

It hadn't brought him near to God, it had left him further from God.

It was this passionate pursuit of anyone who followed Jesus which led him to Damascus. He had heard of a community of followers and wanted to bring them to justice. To arrest them, try them and kill them. On his way to Damascus he describes a bright light and the voice of Jesus asking him

"why are you persecuting Me?"
NIV

Jesus then went on to invite him into relationship with Him. To work in partnership with Him, spreading his newfound story with the whole world. Instead of taking his message of legalism, oppression and death around the world, he now got to take a message of grace, freedom and life.

Same action.
Different heart.

And so Paul left the law behind and chose relationship with God through Jesus. Now he saw the beauty of grace and the ugliness of legalism. He saw the short-comings of law, and the fullness of relationship through grace.

And there was no going back. Paul recognised that the law, the religious system, the legalistic mindset, had failed to reunite him with God.
It had failed to save him.
It had failed to restore him.
It had failed to convince God that he was good enough.

In fact it had rendered him in opposition to the very God he was trying to serve.

This law, which had been given to liberate and transform, had become a weapon of oppression and exclusion. This law which had been about identity, and hope, and life, had become about conformity, fear, and death.

Same law,
different heart.

It had taught him all about God, but had left him worshipping an unknown God. A distortion of God. A misrepresentation of God. It had left him not '*knowing*' God at all.

This law which had been about drawing people closer to God had become a barrier to God. It left people distant and afraid. Not good enough and ashamed. And instead of revealing God as a God of love, and connection, and forgiveness, and life, and inclusion, and beauty, it painted a God of anger, and isolation, and vengeance, and death, and ugliness.

Sound familiar?

Do we find ourselves living under law again?
Do we find ourselves imposing our law on others?
Do we find ourselves using the law to exclude or condemn?
Do we find ourselves becoming proud or judgemental, wanting to correct others, or prove that others aren't following the rules properly, or obeying God properly?
Do we find ourselves using the law to attack people, or control people, or oppress people, or get rid of people?
Do we find ourselves thinking that God hates our enemies as much as we do?
Do we find ourselves thinking of God as angry, or destructive, or vengeful, or distant?
Do we find ourselves being nervous or afraid of God?
Do we find ourselves feeling not good enough or ashamed?
Do we find ourselves thinking we have disappointed God, or that we are being punished by Him?

This is what the law does.

It disconnects us.

It leaves us stuck at the bottom of the mountain and tells us that we aren't good enough.
It leaves God at the top of the mountain furious with us.
Disappointed with us.
Disconnected from us.

So what would happen if we took Paul at his word?

What if we believed him when he said the law is irrelevant? Or that it can't save us? What if we dived into that idea and recognised that not only are we are not under law, but that the law can send us in the wrong direction completely? What if we understood that the law keeps us rooted at the bottom of the mountain and it distorts our view of God, rendering Him distant, and inaccessible?

What if we believed it?

What if instead of being rooted at the bottom of the mountain, weighed down by the law, we were invited to climb up and meet God, with all our failures and shame and mistakes and not good enoughs?

How would we read the Ten Commandments then?

What if we took another look at them, without the stigma, or shame, or fear, or legalism?
What would they say about who God is?
What would they say about who we are and who we are created to be?
What would they say about how we treat others, or see others, or interact with others?
What would they say about life and how we live it?

What if they were all about liberation and not condemnation?

What if they were all about relationship and not rules?

That's what this book is about.

An invitation to know the unknown god.

part 2

commands

first

"I am the Lord your God, who brought you out
of Egypt, out of the land of slavery."
"You shall have no other gods before me."

NIV

first

The first command is all about God.

Which on one level is very simple and on another, very complicated. But it's probably worth considering what we mean when we use the word God.

How we think of God is quite important. We can often fall into the trap of thinking about God in the same way we think about ourselves. By that I mean we think of Him as some sort of man-type figure with super powers. We think of Him as holding the universe, but not in the universe. Sort of the same way I used to play with my toys as a child. I would manipulate them, move them, interact with them, but theirs' was the imaginary world. I was directing it, and influencing it, and choreographing it, and designing it, but I wasn't in it, or part of it.

We see this sort of thinking all over our culture. From friezes on ancient temples, to songs we used to sing in school such as 'He's got the whole world in His hands',
And then there's movies we watch like Superman, Bruce Almighty, and The Devil's Advocate, to name just a few.

In Superman we see all sorts of imagery which connects ideas of God as super-human. Essentially good but profoundly different. From falling to earth in the shape of a crucifix, to battling evil, to saving those in desperate trouble, and even in the latest Batman vs Superman film, hinting at a Messiah rising from the grave.

In Bruce Almighty, God is accused of being a mean kid at an anthill with a magnifying glass burning all the little ants. It tackles ideas of God being able to answer everyones prayers and requests, having files of everything people have done wrong and knowing all there is to know about them. The imagery just keeps coming.

The Devil's Advocate shows Al Pacino as the devil who is trying to recruit his son to have a child who will be the anti-Christ.

In the film there are a couple of monologues which are simply sensational. One of which talks of God sitting up there like the ultimate joker, setting our instincts one way, and all the rules in opposition, for His own cosmic amusement.

God is outside of this realm, this dimension, this reality. Outside of time itself. And yet He sits over it, directing it at will. Interjecting, or interfering as He sees fit. And we are helpless and subject to His whim.

Not a very pleasant idea of God.

But what if God's not like that?

What if God isn't just some sort of super human?

What if God isn't detached and distant?

What if God isn't just a big guy in the sky?

What if God is much,

much,

bigger than that?

buckets

I used to love going to the beach. I didn't get to go very often, but when I did I would take my bucket and spade and try and build the biggest sand castle I could. I grew out of this for a while, until I had my own kids, and then the fascination came back pretty quick.

We would spend ages building huge fancy sandcastles, with numerous turrets around the large walls. On the inside we would build walkways and a central mound with a giant turret on top. It was big enough for us to all stand in. It was a work of art. And then, when we had built it, we would start on the moat. This would be deep and would go all around the castle. Then we would build a ditch, and a wall to try and stop the sea encroaching on our castle. Finally we would try and fill the moat.

 It would take a while.

For ages we would go back and forth to the sea, collecting buckets of water and bringing them back and pouring them into the moat, where they would instantly disappear into the sand. It didn't matter how many buckets we collected, the sea would never get lower and the moat would never get fuller. The only time we would see the moat fill up even slightly is when the sea would overcome our sea defences and wash over the castle.

We would fill dozens, maybe even hundreds of buckets, but it would make little or no difference. The moat would never fill, and the sea would always keep coming. Which leads us to a question.

How many buckets of water are there in the ocean?

Which reminds of a fact I heard. Apparently there are as many atoms in a glass of water as there are glasses of water in the whole ocean.

Stop and think about that for a moment.

Which reminds me of the time I was flying back from Brazil. I fell asleep just as we were leaving the mainland of Brazil and setting out over the ocean. Seven or eight hours later I woke up and we were still over the ocean. All that time. Flying at over five hundred miles an hour. All that water. All those glasses of water.

Staggering.

Which reminds me of another fact I heard.

We have only explored around 5% of the ocean and believe we may only have discovered as little as 10% of the species in the ocean. Which all leads me to a much more philosophical question.

If I fill my bucket with sea water, but then drop it into the sea, is the sea in my bucket or is my bucket in the sea?

Obviously they are both true. However, whilst some of the sea is in the bucket, the whole bucket is in the sea, and so the bucket being in the sea is a much greater truth.

Which may have you wondering what this has to do with God and how we think of God.

If we see God as the sea in this analogy, and myself as the bucket, I can fall into the trap of seeing God as just the sea which is in my bucket. So He is restricted to the size of my imagination, or my capacity to understand, or my experience of Him, or my theology.

But what if God isn't restricted by the shape or size of my bucket? What if God is much bigger than that?

Whilst it is profoundly true that God is in me, what if I realised that it is a much greater truth that I am in God, and God is ridiculously vaster than the size of my experience or my understanding or my theology, or even my imagination?
What if, rather than God being somewhere else and interacting with me from a distance, God entirely surrounded me?
What if God was everywhere?
What if God consumed me?
What if I was entirely saturated by God?
What if my entire existence was in Him?

My ability to breathe.

My ability to love.

My ability to create.

My ability to connect and give and serve.

My capacity for joy and hope and patience and generosity.

My courage to forgive and take steps of faith.

All in Him.

What if God, rather than being some genie I called out to when
I needed something, was an all-consuming, ever-present
reality who was actually

my

source

of

everything.

source

The idea of God as our source of everything is a beautiful and intriguing idea. It is something the writers of scripture are trying to find language for when they talk about God being like breath, and life, and water, and light. A God who shelters me, and a God who knows me. A God who is like air, and fire, and a God who is in the whisper, and on the breeze. A God who is a lover, and a God who is within us. They paint a picture of a God who is omnipresent and ever present. A God who is entwined with every aspect of our life and our universe. A God who is our source of everything.

But what does that look like?

The first commandment is about God for a reason. He is the starting point of everything. He is the beginning. The Alpha. The Genesis. The Creator. The source of everything. In Colossians it says of Christ, that all things were created in Him, everything in heaven and on earth.

It says that God was the beginning of all things, and that all things are held together in Him. Which reminds us of Genesis. And it goes on to say that all things are reconciled in Him. which reminds us of where this is all heading. It paints this beautiful picture of God as the source of all things, and all things are brought together in Him, exist in Him and are restored in Him. God is the source of our life, and our life is reconciled in Him. Without Him we have no life.

Otherwise known as death.

Which makes some sense of the language we see Jesus using when He says, 'I have come that you may have life and life to the full.' It makes sense of the imagery we see in the gospel of moving from death to life. Paul talks of us being dead in our sin, but now being alive in Christ. And he encourages us to be rooted in Christ so that we continue to live our lives in Him.

This imagery of God as the source of life is all over the scriptures.

When we look to God as the source of our life it liberates us from the death that has consumed us. It reconnects us with our creator and the giver of life, and it teaches us to live in harmony and rhythm with Him.

This is what the first commandment is pointing to.

It's not an instruction from a petty or insecure God to prove to Him how much we love Him or worship Him. It's not an order to appease Him, pander to His ego, or avert his anger. It's an invitation into life.

It's an invitation to live the lives we were created to live.

And it's about more than just finding our source of life in Him. It's also an invitation to look to Him for our hope, our security, our identity, our status, and even our purpose or our calling.

What are the things we put our hope in?

I don't know how you answer that question but there must be a wide array of answers. From leaders, to political systems, to family, to qualifications, to property, to money, to sports teams, and the list goes on. But in the Psalms we see the question

> 'where does my hope come from' ?
> NIV

This idea that hope isn't just what we put in the stuff, and people, and the transitory things in our life, but rather that hope 'comes from' somewhere. Hope that comes from the God who spoke creation into existence, God who is pulling the trajectories of all creation towards restoration and justice.

This is all heading somewhere. It's heading somewhere profound and beautiful and whole. Because God isn't just directing from a distance, He **is** the trajectory, and the creation, and the justice, and the restoration. And because I *know* God, I can be confident that this is headed towards a beautiful fulfilment.

And that same God is calling me forward to step into more hope and more of my identity. He is calling me forward to take steps of justice, and wholeness, and restoration, and forgiveness, and beauty, and hope.

However desperate it looks right now.

However messy it is.

However hopeless it feels.

I am part of something so much bigger, and it's headed somewhere profound, and beautiful, and whole.

Now that's hope.

We look to so many things for our security. And not just our own security, but the security of our family. We look to money, pension plans, savings accounts, investment funds, insurance policies, trust funds, rainy day accounts, nest eggs, and the list goes on. All to make sure that we are safe and secure. We buy bigger houses, with bigger gates, and alarm systems, and more land, in better neighbourhoods, and near better schools. Because we can always be better protected. And this doesn't just work on a personal level, it works on a national level too. We spend trillions and trillions on defence to make us feel safer, but we can always feel safer still. Governments make huge shows of strength when national security is threatened by another nation, or a terrorist, or financial markets, or whatever else. We build walls and make threats, and drop bombs, and exclude people, and reinforce our nationalism, or our tribalism. We reassert ourselves, we belittle others, we worry, and stress, and displace our anger, because we can never feel safe enough.

Our identity is fascinating. We put so much effort into creating our image and our identity. From the clothes we buy, to the careers we pursue. The people we want to be associated with or the restaurants we want to be seen in. And we are so tempted by what the better job, or nicer clothes, or classier restaurants would say about us.

And then there's social media, where we spend hours and hours presenting the right image with our comments, our musical taste, the TV and the movies we watch, the shows and concerts we go to, the pets we have, the pictures we post, the religious memes, the political comments, the sporting triumphs. And we can get so worked up about the number of followers and friends we get. The likes and shares we get. The comments and mentions we get.

All of which flows into our status. Which holidays do we go on, which neighbourhood do we live in, which car do we drive, how successful are we? All of which drives us to climb higher, be better, be richer, more successful, have better status symbols, which all costs money. Which means we need more money to feel better, and more successful, and more popular, and more secure, and more fulfilled. And so it goes on. It's a stressful cycle to be stuck on. Which in turn leads to those bigger questions.
Why am I here?
What am I supposed to be doing?

and who am I?

Questions which we attempt to answer with a range of things such as fame or family, or career, or enjoyment of life, or whatever else might make us feel fulfilled. Which brings us back to Jesus saying 'I have come that you may have life in all its fullness'.

Which brings us back to God as the source of life, and hope, and security, and identity, and status and purpose.

What if we understood how to live fully, in harmony and rhythm with the source of life Himself? What if life wasn't something we chased after, or tried to achieve? What if life was something that flowed through us in the good times and the bad? In success and in failure? What if life was something that we didn't just enjoy, but something that we brought to a room, or a family, or a workplace, or a community, or a city? What if the source of life flowed through us and changed the world around us?

What if our security didn't come from money or assets, or power or might? What if our security came from knowing who we are and whose we are? What if we didn't have to prove ourselves and exert our rights or our superiority? What if our security came from knowing our creator, and the confidence and contentment that brings? What if our security came from knowing we were held together by the God that holds all things together?

What if identity wasn't something we tried to create and cultivate, but something we came to discover and uncover, as we plunged deeper and deeper into our relationship with the Father? What if our identity was rooted in the idea that we are created by the source of all things?

Loved by Love Himself.
Children of the God of life.
Co-heirs with Christ.
Living in the fullness of who God created us to be.
People who bless and change the world around us.

What if our status wasn't bought or found in titles or careers, but rather in being accepted by the Father of all creation? Being loved and in relationship with the God of the universe. People who move and operate in the power and influence of the God who flows through us, People who bring healing and hope and life and beauty to the world around us.

What if our purpose and our calling wasn't just a ubiquitous question about the meaning of life, but rather a deeply discovered realisation of who we were created to be?

A purpose that doesn't just make sense of the questions, but a purpose that makes sense of ourselves completely.
A purpose that makes sense of the world.
A purpose that changes the world around you.
A purpose that was invested in you at the source of all creation, by the source of all creation.
A purpose that makes sense of you.

But here's the rub

Where we seek any of these things from the world around us, whether that be money, or career, or status symbols, or people's praise, or family, or property, or experiences, or toys, or whatever it might be, we always want more.

We can always feel more secure. We can always need more hope. We can always have better status symbols, or a higher profile, or more success, or a bigger house, or more savings, or a better family. We can always be more popular or famous or do more, achieve more, or earn more, or win more, and so we become insatiable.

We become addicted.

Always wanting more.
Always 25% away from having enough.

And so we become consumers.
Insatiable consumers.
Addicted consumers.
Dissatisfied, frustrated consumers.

But we weren't created to be consumers.

We were created to be givers.

We were created to be a blessing to the world.

And so here's the beautiful thing.

As we learn to look to God as our source of life, hope, security, identity, status and purpose, so we learn that not only are we enough, but that we have enough.

We aren't living in scarcity, we are living in enough.
We are living in plenty.
We are living in abundance.

And so we are free to give.

We are free to be a blessing, because God is a constant source of life, and security, and blessing, and hope, and purpose, and identity.

And so we share.

We open our homes, we look to those who have less and we live generously. We give and we bless, and we build others up. We encourage, we cheer on, we join in, we let ourselves be seen, and we reflect the God we were created to reflect.

Which brings us on to the second commandment.

second

"You shall not make for yourself an image in the form of anything in heaven above or on the earth beneath or in the waters below. You shall not bow down to them or worship them; for I, the Lord your God, am a jealous God, punishing the children for the sin of the parents to the third and fourth generation of those who hate me, but showing love to a thousand generations of those who love me and keep my commandments."

NIV

genesis

Everything starts in Genesis.

This is an important understanding, and it's pivotal to how we read scripture. So often we tend to quote verses or stories from scripture to back up our point, and claim that because it is in the Bible, it is therefore unquestionable.

The problem is that this approach has been used to support all sorts of viewpoints, some of them quite violent or oppressive or exclusive. Which is fine if that is what God is like. But what if God's not like that and we just used scripture to prove that God agreed with us? What if we used scripture to attack people? What if we used scripture to keep slaves in line? Or women, or children, or congregations, or whoever? Or what if we used scripture to keep others out?

There's a story about a guy seeking inspiration from God about what he should do in a certain situation. He takes the tried and tested model of randomly opening his Bible, closing his eyes and pointing to a section on the page, opening his eyes and reading it, as a way of letting the Spirit guide him and direct him. You may laugh, and I wouldn't blame you, but I have done this myself on more than one occasion. Sometimes God seems to have used it and sometimes I have just been very confused.

Anyway, back to the story. On this occasion the man followed the formula and happened upon Matthew 27:5

> 'So Judas threw the money into the temple and left.
> Then he went and hanged himself.'
>
> NIV

A little unnerved but fairly certain that God didn't want him to hang himself, he decided to try again. This time he found Luke 10:37

> 'Go and do likewise.'
> NIV

You see, it's a risky game taking random verses and applying 'God says' to them for your own particular situation.

Similarly it is risky taking something that is written for a specific circumstance and making it a universal truth. Sometimes we do this with verses from scripture, when the text or context doesn't really merit it. Some of the statements in Paul's letters are a good example. Paul is writing at a specific time, to specific people about a specific issue that has arisen. It can be risky for us to take a line from one of these letters and declare it to be a universal truth.

At one point Paul wishes someone would castrate themselves. At another he instructs women to be quiet in a particular situation, and in another he calls all Cretans (I.e. people from the island of Crete) liars, evil brutes, lazy and gluttons.

So it is important that we understand the bigger picture, the big story, so we can understand the details within the stories. The big story we think is being told, defines how we understand the details within the story.

Have you ever watched a film, which is heading in a particular direction, when suddenly it seems to go in a totally different direction. or be a totally different type of film. Sometimes a thriller can become a farce, or a horror can become a comedy, or a romance can become quite dark, and it throws us. It makes us rethink the whole film, or sometimes we can just give up and feel let down.

Because the big story matters.

And this is true in life too.

The story we think we live in defines our behaviour.

The way we see the world defines how we interact with the world.

I

If we believe a story that says that God is going to destroy the earth one day, and just before He does He will save the souls of those who believed in Him, then that might lead us to a certain set of values. Values that say the earth is expendable, it's all going to burn one day, so it doesn't matter what we do to it.

Which could lead to us acting quite irresponsibly towards the planet, or being unconcerned by global warming and the impact that has on people in poverty around the world.

Values that say the only thing that really matters about a person is their soul and whether or not it is going to heaven. So it doesn't matter about someone's physical state, social state, their welfare, their mental well being, or emotional state or anything else. The only thing that matters about anyone is their soul and whether they have made the right decision.

Which could leave us showing quite a lack of concern or care to someone who is starving, or sick or depressed. It could lead to us not engaging in issues of social justice, or social breakdown.

This is just one example of the sort of story we might think we live in. There are many. Multitudes. As there are many ideas of what God is like. And that's not just true for those who believe in God. Even atheists have rejected a definition of a god they don't believe in. Often it relates directly to the sort of god they were 'sold' as a child, or it is influenced by the culturally dominant idea of god.

Often its an arbitrary, cruel, distant god, who decides who lives and who dies, who suffers and who doesn't, which diseases to create or allow, and which to not. Who to save and who to abandon.

Sometimes it's a god who demands to be loved or worshipped or adored, but with seemingly few appealing characteristics that would inspire that adoration or worship or love within us.

Sometimes it's a god who incites hatred and war, even demanding it, causing untold suffering.

Quite reasonably these narratives can cause people to disconnect from the idea of God, even being quite offended by the idea that anyone could choose to believe or engage with that narrative, or that God.

So the story we live in is important.

It is important that we have an understanding of what God is like, so that when we read scripture we can pick up the themes and threads of God. It's important that we are able to detect the DNA or heartbeat of God. That we are able to uncover and explore the mysteries.
And so it is important that we look to the beginning of the story to discover those threads. The trajectories that will course through scripture and point towards an ultimate destination. An ultimate goal.

But as I say, it all starts in Genesis.

visible

As we have already seen, Genesis reveals God to be a creator God. A God who speaks life, creates space and fills it with vibrancy. A God who invites us to join in. And in Genesis 1 God says

'let us make mankind in our image, in our likeness, so that they may rule over the fish and the sea and the birds in the sky, over the livestock and all the wild animals, and over all the creatures that move along the ground.'

NIV

We will come back to the 'us' part of that later, but the Hebrew word used here for 'image' is 'tselem', which is the same word used later in scripture for graven images. A graven image, or idol, was a very common thing in the Old Testament era. Every family would have their gods that they worshipped, and so they would have a shrine in their home with carved images of their gods. These idols or images, were visible representations of the invisible god. They would carry a likeness of the god, and demonstrate some of the characteristics. It wasn't the god itself, but it represented the god and its power.

In the same way God made man in His image. As a visible image or representation of the invisible God. As a representative to the world of God himself, demonstrating God's characteristics, carrying some of God's authority and power to have authority over the earth and its inhabitants. This is the story we see in Genesis. Man being the visible representative of the invisible God. He is tasked with naming the animals, which is an action of authority, calling out the identity and character of each species. And he is to rule the earth and all the animals of the earth and birds of the sky and fish in the sea.

Man is to represent God's authority ,and rule like God over the earth.

God has delegated.

The problem is that man decided it wasn't enough to rule like God and be the visible representation of God on the earth. He decided he wanted to BE God. And so he went his own way. Living in opposition to God. Living in rebellion to God. Living disconnected from God. And ironically, living less human lives than God had intended.

But God had a plan. God calls out Abraham and calls him to leave the security, and identity, and life of his homeland and instead go with God. He would rise up into a family, a tribe and a nation that would be a blessing to the whole world. Because God always blesses us to be a blessing to the world. Abraham, and his family would show the world something of what God was like, but it was going to be a long journey.

in Genesis we see Abraham's great grandson, Joseph, helping whole nations survive a famine, and revealing God to be a God of blessing and provision and compassion and generosity.

Exodus is the story of how God saves His people from slavery, revealing God to be a God who hears the cry of His people. A God who saves the oppressed. And when He saves them and brings them out of Egypt, He reminds them of their calling. He calls them a kingdom of priests. A priest is someone who represents God to the people. A visible representation of the invisible God, revealing something of what God is like. And here God is referring to them as a nation of priests. This is a community calling. A national calling. That the world should be able to look at them and see something of what God is like. Their national calling is to be a light and a blessing to the world.

The irony that we see as they continue their journey is, that often the nations and tribes around them do see that God is with Israel and blessing them, but Israel themselves seem less sure. The Israelites are afraid of Jericho, but when they finally muster up the courage to spy on the city, they discover that the people of Jericho have been convinced of God's greatness for years, and they know He is with Israel. Again when they enter the promised land, they encounter people who have been more than aware of Israel's God for a long time.

How often do we fail to see God at work in us and in our situation, and it takes others to point it out to us?

As we continue through the Old Testament, we encounter story after story of Israel forgetting their own story and failing to live the lives God is calling them to. And so time and again we see God sending prophets to remind them of their calling. In Isaiah we see God reminding His people to be a light to the nations. To show the world what God is like, and to invite the world towards paths of restoration and life. And God says that it is not enough to restore Israel to their calling as God's people, this light is for the whole world.

This is for everyone.

God is moving beyond the idea of a personal God, a family God, a tribal God or even a national God. God is declaring Himself to be God of the whole world, and promises that one is coming who will draw all the earth towards Himself.

Cue Jesus.

Colossians 1

'The Son is the image of the invisible God, the first-born over all creation. For in him all things were created: things in heaven and on earth, visible and invisible, whether thrones or powers or rulers or authorities; all things have been created through him and for him. He is before all things, and in him all things hold together. And he is the head of the body, the church; he is the beginning and the first-born from among the dead, so that in everything he might have the supremacy. For God was pleased to have all his fullness dwell in him, and through him to reconcile to himself all things, whether things on earth or things in heaven, by making peace through his blood, shed on the cross.

Once you were alienated from God and were enemies in your minds because of your evil behaviour. But now he has reconciled you by Christ's physical body through death to present you holy in his sight, without blemish and free from accusation— if you continue in your faith, established and firm, and do not move from the hope held out in the gospel. This is the gospel that you heard and that has been proclaimed to every creature under heaven, and of which I, Paul, have become a servant.'

NIV

Jesus

Jesus is introduced to us in Mark at His baptism. Heaven is ripped open, a dove descends on Him, and a voice from heaven says
'You are my Son, whom I love; with you I am well pleased'
NIV

That is quite the entry, and quite the endorsement.

Jesus goes on to say things like,
'If you have seen me then you have seen the Father'
and 'I am the light of the world'
and 'No-one comes to the Father except through me'.
NIV

This is verbalised perfectly in Colossians 1:15,
'The Son is the image of the invisible God.'
NIV

The role we were created for has now been fulfilled in Christ. Jesus is the fullest revelation of what God is like. For centuries, man has been grasping and wrestling with ideas of what God is like, and then, as it so beautifully puts it in the Message,

'God moved into the neighbourhood'.

Jesus comes to reveal to us exactly what God is like, and the surprising thing is, it's not what anybody was expecting. In fact it's probably fair to say that Jesus' principle message was

God's not like that.

The Israelites were expecting a Messiah. They had understood the scriptures to say that one was coming who would save them. One who would restore Israel to its calling, and be a light to the nations, which is exactly what Jesus did, except it didn't look anything like they expected. The expectation was that this Messiah would overthrow their enemies, free them from the oppression of the Roman empire and the immorality of the Greek empire, and restore God's glory in the Temple in Jerusalem. They believed He would glorify and raise up the religious leaders of Israel for maintaining the law of the Old Testament in Israel, and all nations would come to Jerusalem, from all over the world, to marvel at His power and the beauty of the Temple and Israel.

So it's fair to say, things didn't go quite to plan.

There was a fear of God, and a belief that if you saw the face of God you would die. This was such a strong belief that the once a year a priest would go into the holy of holies, the inner sanctum of the Temple. He would enter with a rope tied around him, so that should he die, they could pull him out again without having to go inside. All this was part of an elaborate temple system which was all in place to keep God holy and separate. Only the Jews could enter the temple, and even then, only the good enough Jews who had paid their offerings, made their sacrifices and received the costly blessing of the religious leaders to say they had kept the laws.

All this meant that many Jews couldn't go in the temple. Jews who were sick, or who hadn't paid their taxes, or tithes, or couldn't afford the various extortionate costs of blessings, or sacrifices or whatever else kept the poor on the outside. Women who were menstruating, or people seen to be colluding with the Roman occupiers such as tax collectors also couldn't go in, people who didn't wear the right clothes, or obey the right rules. God was exclusive, God was angry and petty, and God was distant. So much so that He was really only talked about in the past or future tenses.

All the tales were of the great stories of Israel's past, such as parting the Red Sea, and defeating Jericho, and stories of the great victories they had won hundreds of years before. Or they were stories of what was going to happen when God came back. How Israel's enemies were going to be thrown into the sea. How the Temple was going to be fully restored, even beyond its former beauty. Stories of how the Messiah would ride into Jerusalem on a donkey and God's Kingdom would be established on earth, in Jerusalem for all the world to see.

Great stories of the past and the future, but nothing of the present, because God was nowhere to be seen, or heard, or known.

And then Jesus came. And the angels called Him Immanuel, which means God with us.

No longer distant, or silent, now God was with us, and could be known directly and personally. Now He could be seen and heard, teaching people about what God is like, performing miracles such as healing the sick, making the blind see, the deaf hear, the dead come back to life. He confronted the spiritual powers, and quite shockingly, associated the demonic powers with the religious system. suggesting that control and power were at the centre of the religious system that oppressed and excluded. He confronted the religious leaders, and their systems of blessings and offerings and sacrifices and called them children of the devil. He condemned them for how they treated the poor and the sick.

Rather than endorsing the religious system, He tore it down.

Rather than being holy and separate from the sinners, he directly associated himself with the sick, and the tax collectors and the sinners. So much so that it's fair to say that Jesus evicted God from the temple and poured Him out into the streets, the gutters and the brothels, to be with the unclean, the outcast and the lost. And rather than punishing the sinners, he started declaring them forgiven. He included the children, and the ostracised and the others, and the foreigner. Rather than being the God who would kill you if you saw Him, Jesus drew people to Him, and when He came face to face with a dead person, invariably they came back to life.

Jesus also spent time outside of Israel, in the Greek and Roman towns of the region, healing the sick, feeding the masses, raising the dead, and demonstrating that rather than coming to overthrow Israel's enemies and throw them into the sea, it was the pigs that He threw into the sea as an act of liberation for the other nations.

Jesus reveals to us a quite different God.

A God who isn't like that. Jesus reveals to us a God who is restoring all things back to himself. A God who is restoring heaven and earth. A God who is announcing a new Kingdom, a new relationship, and He is inviting us to join in.

This Kingdom Jesus was announcing had room for everyone.

This wasn't a God of anger, but of love.

This wasn't a God of exclusivity, but of inclusivity.

This wasn't a God of history, but of the present.

This wasn't a God of wrath, but of forgiveness.

This wasn't a God of death, but of life.

This wasn't a God of power, but of weakness.

This God wasn't against us, this God was for us.

This God wasn't inaccessible, this God was vulnerable.

This wasn't a God who demanded sacrifices,

this was a God who was the sacrifice.

us

When I was a teenager I would from time to time check myself off against the Ten Commandments. I would go through the list and tick the ones I was keeping. I would often tick the first command as one I kept, although there were definitely times I wasn't so sure, but the second command was always an easy tick. Whilst I might question whether I had other gods such as Manchester United, girlfriends, or whatever was the trend at the time, I never had any questions about having any idols or graven images. It just wasn't something that I did. I would often be confused why it was there. Not only did it seem quite irrelevant to me in the 20th century, it seemed like duplication. Surely idols could be considered a god and so included in the first commandment.

There were other commands that were clearly achieved if I took them literally. Adultery and murder were things I managed to steer clear from. I didn't tend to covet my neighbours ass, ox or slaves, but the command to not have idols was always my easiest tick.

The problem is that I had really misunderstood it.

Whilst the first command is all about God being God, the second command is more about us being us.

Where the first command is about God taking His rightful place, the second is about us taking our rightful place.

Where the first command is all about God being the source of life, security, identity, purpose and status, then the second is all about us being conduits of that blessing to the world, as image bearers and representatives of that God in the world.

Let's go back to that story that we live in, and why God says let 'us' make mankind in 'our' image.

Often we can think of God as distant and arbitrary. A big guy in the sky who administers His judgement as He sees fit. But Genesis paints a different picture. Genesis shows God as an interdependent relational God. A God who is in relationship with Himself, and a God who is in relationship with mankind. We see imagery of God walking in the garden, talking to man, which tells a tale of a God not distant but intimate.
Not arbitrary but relational.
And God invites us to participate in creation, and to participate in life with Him. We are God's plan for creation. But as we have seen, we choose to go our own way. Instead of looking to God for our life, purpose, hope, identity and so much more, we choose to go it alone and to find those things in creation.

This is a huge disconnection.

When I was a child I was told about how our sin had caused a division between us and God, and that is certainly true, but it is even more catastrophic than that. To suggest the only problem I have is a disconnection between me and God, which can be resolved by a prayer inviting Him into my heart is to undersell the problem, and the solution offered by Jesus, massively.

We suffer profound disconnection in every aspect of our being.

Genesis tells a story of profound disconnection between us as humans. A deep relational disconnect that means relationships will be about power and control now. There will be a distrust between us. Things hidden. We will blame each other, oppress each other, abuse each other, overpower each other, be at war with each other, hate each other and dehumanise each other.

Similarly we will be at odds with God. Deeply disconnected from our creator, resulting in us being less human than we were created to be. Rather than being in beautiful relationship with our creator, we will strive to be gods ourselves. We will look elsewhere to determine our identity, our security, our status, our calling and our life. We will look to find fulfilment and purpose through all sorts of means other than God. And because we can never be enough, or have enough, or be safe enough, or be fulfilled enough or be content, we will be persistent and perpetual consumers.

All of this will be driven by a deep inner disconnect. An underlying shame and conviction that we are not good enough can see us turn to all sorts of measures to numb that pain and sense of loss. We learn to project who we want to believe we are, and who we want the world to believe we are, whilst being deeply aware that it's not true, and live in varying states of fear that we will be found out.

This can be exacerbated by an irrational conviction that everyone else has this sorted, which can lead to us pouring all sorts of energy into trying to be someone else, or idolising someone else, or choosing to follow someone who appears to have answers to our inner pain.

In addition to all this we suffer a disconnection from creation itself. Instead of being in complete harmony with creation, we go to extreme lengths to coerce creation to our own ends. We find ourselves in struggle with creation, even to the extent that we see it merely as a resource to be controlled and harnessed for our profit, rather than a dynamic creation to find rhythms of harmony with.

This is something we will look at in more detail later, but for now it's important to see that the Bible tells this story of deep disconnection in us and between us and around us, and between us and God.

But that's not the end of the story.

The good news is that the rest of the Bible tells the story of God seeking to restore all things.

All creation.
All of us.
All relationships.
All identities.
All sickness and death, and hate, and enmity, and fear, and pain and despair, and deception.

All things.

Everything. To Him.

Scripture paints a picture of trajectories of love and hope and sacrifice wrestling heaven and earth back together again. Inviting us to paths of restoration and wholeness.

A story that shows God interacting again and again with His creation and His people to reverse the tide of disconnection that's flowing through history.

A story that has Jesus at the centre.

A story that invites us to reconnect in every way we can.

And Jesus announces a new kingdom.
A turn in the tide.
A new movement towards heaven and earth being restored.

And He invites us to join in.

We are His body. A visible representation of Him. His image bearers. People who collectively show the world what He is like. People who will look again to Him for their identity as children of God. Co-heirs with Christ. Agents of the Kingdom of God.
People who will look to Him for their life, and their purpose.
People who will be a blessing to the world.
People who will reconnect with God and reconnect with their God given identity,
People who will reconnect with their family, and their neighbour and their enemy.
People who will reconnect with creation and find rhythms of joy and harmony, recognising their creator in every person and every corner of creation.
People who carry a deep, confident hope that God is in all things, and all things are ultimately coming together in Christ, and we are part of that story, created to be a blessing to the whole world around us.

Imagine if we lived in that story.

How would that change our behaviour?

children

The second part of this command is quite troubling. The idea of God punishing our children to the third and fourth generation just because we broke this command.
What does it say about God that he would punish our children for our mistakes? That sounds like quite a cruel and vindictive God. A God of threats and coercion. A self proclaimed jealous God who will take our mistakes out on our children, grandchildren, great grandchildren and even great great grandchildren.

What is that even about? And how does that relate to Jesus who said 'let the children come to me' and also said that the parents' sins wouldn't be passed down on to their children.

As my niece would say 'What the even heck God?'

This is another of the problems when we take a legalistic view of the commandments. If they are rules to be kept, and breaking one of them results in not just us being punished, but our children too, then that makes God cruel and vindictive. But if we view them as a comment, or revelation of who God is, who we are and how life works, then maybe they take on a different tone.

If we understand that sin is about all the ways in which we are disconnected and dehumanised, then it puts this passage in a different light. It tells a story of a disconnection that occurs when we live in opposition to the nature and character of God. It tells of a dehumanisation that takes place when we don't act as the image bearers of God.

The consequence of that isn't an arbitrary punishment delivered down to us by an angry God, but rather a natural relational, societal and cultural consequence that isn't just restricted to me or even my generation or moment in time, but one that flows down through the generations. My actions don't just disconnect and dehumanise me, but also my family, and my children, and their children. My generation and the ones to follow. The things that are done to me, the culture I grow up in, and the society I am part of, form me and distort me. And unless I choose to name it, recognise it, confront it and confess it, I will pass that on to the next generation and the next.

How often do we see this play out in front of us. We see cycles of behaviour being passed on. Cycles of addiction, cycles of abuse, cycles of greed, cycles of poverty, cycles of depression, cycles of self esteem, cycles of power, cycles of control, cycles of fear, cycles of hate and enmity and jealousy and anger and adultery and dishonesty and crime and cycles of violence. Passed on from generation to generation. Consequences of choices made by previous generations building itself into the DNA of a family for generations. A seemingly unbreakable chain that goes on from generation after generation.

And these cycles become rooted in us and empower systems that perpetuate that greed, or poverty, or disempowerment, or violence or crime, or hate and the list goes on.

But God, rather than being the God who delivers this sentence to us, is the God who offers to deliver us from this cycle and these systems.
God, rather than being the God who punishes our children, is the one who invites us to break the chain and liberate our children. Rather than being the God who condemns us to death, He is the God who implores us to choose life.

Which is why, when Jesus comes, He challenges the systems which produce poverty and oppression. He breaks the hold that death has on us and invites us into life. He invites us to live like children in the kingdom, not living under an oppressive law that keeps us fearfully distant from God, but rather deeply connected with the Father, living lives of love in the fullness of our humanity.

And what's more, He invites us to pass that life on, saying that when we live in harmony with Him, the blessing will flow through thousands of generations. A life of blessing rather than curses. Life rather than death. Hope rather than despair. A blessing that will flow through the ages for eternity.

Because that's what God is like.

third

'You shall not misuse the name of the Lord your God, for the Lord will not hold anyone guiltless who misuses His name.'

NIV

jehovah

The third command is one that has been subject to a large amount of misunderstanding. As a law, it has been widely understood to be about what we could and could not say. Specifically what we could or could not say about God. Most notably His name.

In the film 'Life of Brian' there is a famous scene where a man is being stoned for saying the name of God. The stoning was depicted as a scene of entertainment in the film, and so it shows traders selling a variety of stones perfect for a good stoning. It also has stalls selling beards so women could pretend to be men and so gain access to the stoning which was an all male affair. The crowd is baying for blood and desperate to get the stoning underway. So much so that the High Priest is struggling to maintain order. When asked if he has anything to say for himself, the man explains that he was just complimenting his wife on the meal she had cooked saying it was worthy of Jehovah himself. Screams from the crowd go up as he says the name Jehovah and rocks start flying in. The High Priest is outraged but stops the premature stoning so he can finish his reading of the legal statement. The farce continues until the priest himself unwittingly warns the man not to say Jehovah again and is instantly stoned to death himself.

I remember a conversation as a child, between my Mother and her twin sister. One of them had been reading about how the term 'Oh gosh' had evolved from the term 'Oh God' and essentially meant the same thing. Now this was a problem because both my mother and my aunt used to say 'Oh Gosh' an awful lot.

I don't think I ever heard them say it again after that conversation. I remember thinking that this was somehow quite ridiculous. If they didn't know it was linked to 'Oh God' then how could it be wrong for them to say it? Was God really that petty or irrational? And now they knew, did that suddenly make it wrong to say it? And if knowing it was the thing that made it bad, then had my aunt helped my mum or really not helped my mum by telling her what she had read.

Had she made her a sinner by sharing her discovery?

And if that's what it took to upset God or be sentenced to Hell then what does that say about what God is like?

It certainly didn't sound like a God who wanted to be known.

name

Our first child was something of a surprise.
He certainly wasn't planned, but that's not so unusual. What was unusual was that we didn't know he was coming until pretty late on. And when I say pretty late,

I mean late.

Rachel decided to take a pregnancy test when her stomach was a little bloated one weekend, and she noticed some movement. When the test was positive, she went to the doctor who confirmed she was indeed pregnant. Maybe even four months. I should state at this point that whilst there is something of a bump, she is still in her size 8 jeans and her usual petite self.

She went for her first scan three weeks later, and now the bump is bigger having grown quite dramatically in the time between. Whilst having her scan, the nurse asked why she had left her first scan so late. Rachel explained her story and threw an off the cuff remark out there of 'But its not too late, only a couple of months'

The nurse stopped and looked at her with a slightly confused look on her face, and asked, 'How pregnant do you think you are?'
'Five months' replied Rachel.
'Oh' the nurse's face dropped a little. 'I think you're a little further on than that'
'OK' said Rachel nervously, 'How pregnant am I?'

'Well don't go anywhere,' quipped the nurse as gently as she could, 'you're due tomorrow!'

Our son was born a few days later and was 8lbs 6oz. We named our new baby son Jacob, which means deceiver, because he totally fooled us throughout his whole pregnancy.

The story of Jacob in the Bible is also a story of deception and the importance of names. Jacob was the younger, smaller and weaker of two twins. His brother Esau was a hairy strong beast of a man, and Jacob was quite the opposite. When his father was dying, it came time for him to pass on his birthright and blessing. Esau went out to hunt for an appropriate offering to his father so he could receive his blessing, but whilst he was out, Jacob fooled his blind father into thinking he was Esau, and so stole his brother's birthright and blessing.

Jacob promptly ran away to avoid his brothers revenge, and made a life for himself in exile, amassing family and wealth. Years later the time came for him to return to his homeland and meet Esau, and Jacob was nervous. He sent his servants, cattle, possessions and even his family ahead of him until it was just him, alone, waiting to cross the river into his homeland.

At this point we see a very strange story.

Jacob is set upon by a man in the middle of the night and they wrestle until the morning. In the morning, the man asks Jacob to let him go, but Jacob refuses until the man has blessed him.

Because Jacob is always after the blessing.

The man asks Jacob his name, to which Jacob replies 'Jacob'. Then the man says that he is no longer Jacob, but instead will be called Israel which means 'wrestles with God'. Which is all really strange until you realise that the man is God, which then makes it strange in a whole new way. The fascinating thing about this is, the last time we see Jacob being asked his name is in front of his father when he pretends to be Esau. The moment of his theft, his deception, his sin. And so now God is asking him,

'Who are you?'

A deep, soul-searching question of identity. Jacob replies saying 'Jacob', which means liar, deceiver and cheat.

This isn't just an introductory conversation for Jacob. This is a moment of confession. A moment of self realisation. A moment of release of a shame that he has been carrying for years.

And God's response is beautiful.

God gives him a new name.

God says to Jacob that he won't be called Jacob any more, but instead will be called Israel meaning 'wrestles with God'.

How beautiful.

Jacob won't be known as liar and deceiver and cheat any more. He has a new name. a new story. God's response isn't a response of condemnation or shame, it is a response of liberation from his past. An invitation into a new story and a new identity.

All of this to say that names matter in the Bible. It might seem a little odd to us in the 21st century, but names weren't just a name that we liked, or shared with a famous celebrity, or sounded cool. Names in the Bible spoke of the person's story and character. They called out their identity. Which is why we see God changing people's names on some occasions.

Because their story has changed.
God is calling out a new identity in them.

And the same is true today.

When we encounter God up close, and let Him see into our souls, the invitation is always one of liberation and hope.

Liberation from the things that have defined us, or distorted us.

Liberation from things that have been spoken over us, or things we have spoken over ourselves.

Liberation from names we have called ourselves, or limitations we have spoken over ourselves.

Liberation from words of criticism or blame spoken over us by our parents, or family, or partners or friends.

Liberation from shame over things we have done or things that have been done to us.

And when God asks us,

'Who are you?'

we are invited to speak these things out.

To confess them,
admit them,
own up to them,
or name them.

And when we do,

God meets us right there.

And offers us a new name.
A new story.
A new beginning.

A life that isn't restricted any more.
A life that isn't defined by shame or curses.
A life that isn't defined by 'not enough' or lack.
A life that is defined by hope and opportunity.
A life that is defined by acceptance.
A life that is defined by the ultimate life-giver.
A life of invitation, adventure, vulnerability and love.
A life that makes sense of who we are.
A life that is lived to the full.

hypocrites

When we understand how the idea of names works in the Bible, it helps us understand this third command. For so much of my childhood, and beyond, this command was all about what I said, or more accurately, what I didn't say.

But in reality this command isn't about what I say.

It is all about what I do.

This command was all about not saying 'Oh God' or 'Jesus Christ' as some sort of expletive. It meshed in with not swearing, which meant that as a child growing up on the terraces of Old Trafford, there were all sorts of songs I couldn't sing, or at least had to miss whole lines out of. But that is a profound misunderstanding of this command. What we say is important, and it is essential that we use our words to bless and encourage and express truth, but this command is about so much more than that.

The original Hebrew literally means 'do not take upon yourself the 'name' of God and then leave it empty' or ' then live in opposition to it'.

So this is talking about taking upon ourselves the name of God. Or, as we might now understand it, the character or story of God. Because the name of God in the Bible also tells of His character, nature, identity and story. And we see many names for God in the Bible. We see God as creator. God as Father. God as Spirit. God as love. God as life. God as truth. God who protects. God who goes ahead of us. God with us. God who saves. God who judges. God who commands. and we see God call himself I AM WHO I AM. The name which cannot be spoken, and yet is always spoken by all creation. And this is just a selection of the names that speak of God's identity, story and character.

A God who wants to be known.

A God of relationship and connection.

And so this command says that we should not put ourselves in the position of identifying ourselves as God's people, or the image of the invisible God, and then live in ways that are not in keeping with that character or story.

So if God is about love, restoration, forgiveness, hope, beauty, life, truth (and the list goes on), then do not say that we are followers of that God, identified as representatives of that God, or witnesses of that God, and then live lives that are about hate, or division, or resentment, or despair, or rejection, or death, or deceit or prejudice.

If God is about connection and relationship and unity, then do not say we represent and reflect that God and at the same time live lives of disconnection, disagreement and disunity.

We are created to be image-bearers of God. To show the world something of what God is like, the visible image of the invisible God. So let's not be people who affirm this calling, but don't live it out.

Let's not call ourselves followers of Christ and then live lives that are about power, or control, or oppression, or exclusivity.

Let's not call ourselves Christians and then live lives that support those who mock others, torture others, boast, deceive, oppress and exclude others.

Let's not be people who say that we worship a God who loves the whole world, and then live lives that promote nationalism, war, tribalism, and competition.

Let's not be people who say we worship a God who created all things, and provides for all, and then live lives of greed, consumerism, and environmental abuse.

Let's not call ourselves children of God and live lives that promote religious or racial or sexual oppression, child labour, slavery or abuses of human rights.

Let's not call ourselves friends of Jesus and not stand with the poor, the hungry, the refugee, the voiceless, the orphan, the widow or the sick.

Because when we do, we take the name of the Lord
upon us, and live in opposition to it.

We leave it empty.

We become hypocrites.

fourth

'Remember the Sabbath day by keeping it holy. Six days you shall labour and do all your work, but the seventh day is a Sabbath to the Lord your God. On it you shall not do any work, neither you, nor your son or daughter, nor your male or female servant, nor your animals, nor any foreigner residing in your towns. For in six days the Lord made the heavens and the earth, the sea, and all that is in them, but he rested on the seventh day. Therefore the Lord blessed the Sabbath day and made it holy.'

NIV

Sabbath

When I was growing up, Sundays were busy.

We would be up, dressed smart, and at church for nine. Then we would set up the church. I would be helping my Mum, or when I was older, manning the sound desk for the morning meeting. This would run from ten until twelve and then we would play or hang out for an hour whilst Mum and Dad chatted to people. Then we would go home and have a roast dinner, wash up, and then back to church for Sunday school which ran from four until six. Then at six thirty we would have the evening meeting where again I would be on sound. This would run until eight, when we would return home for a thing called round-up which was like a big small group for anyone who wanted to come back after church and do a Bible study, sit around, chat, drink coffee and sing songs.

Not exactly relaxing.

Fast forward to today, and I lead a church, and my kids would tell a not dissimilar, although slightly less frantic story.

So what is Sabbath?
Why is God so insistent on it?
And what does it look like today?

Sabbath is an invitation, or an instruction to rest.

I say instruction because the Israelites were coming from a culture where they weren't used to resting.

Slavery in Egypt was tough.

Always being pushed to do more, achieve more, build more, make more. It was exhausting and dehumanising. Life for them was incessant. From dawn till dusk, being driven and driven to achieve more and more.

Non stop.
Every day.
Every hour.
Every moment.

All of them.
Men.
Women.
Children.
Elderly.

Everyone.

Constantly.

And there was no chance to stop, or breathe, or take stock, or work through their emotion, or loss, or pain, or fear. No chance to contemplate the meaning of life, or the future, or their children's future, or what sort of world they wanted their children to inherit, or anything else because they had no say in that. Their future was set.

And so, as we have seen, as God brings them out of slavery in Egypt, He doesn't just save them geographically, He has to save them socially, spiritually and culturally too.

And so He invites them to rest.

He invites them to stop once a week and breathe.

And not just as individuals, but as a whole community.

And not just the privileged, but the servants, and the children, and the animals, and the immigrants, and the refugees, and the slaves, and the foreigners, and the people of other faith too.

Everyone.

At the same time.

This wasn't just about getting other people to do stuff for you instead, because that doesn't stop our minds. It doesn't still our souls. It doesn't rest our spirits. Nor does it build community, or recognition of the other, or social cohesion.

This was a whole community coming to rest.

A whole tribe.

A whole nation.

Every week.

Coming to rest.

Breathing.

Being.

Still.

Sabbath.

breathe

In your life time you will breathe out the exact same number of times you breathe in.
So the more you breathe in, the more you will need to breathe out. And the more you breathe out, the more you will need to breathe in. It's a biological truth.

And you're very welcome.

But

It's a spiritual truth too.

God is our source. He is our source of life, hope, love, truth and perspective. He is our source of identity, purpose, security and blessing. But we aren't just created to be recipients of these things from God, we're created to be conduits of them to the world around us. We are not just supposed to breathe these things in, we are supposed to breathe them out also. And the more we breathe them in, the more we need to breathe them out. And the more we breathe them out, the more we need to breathe God in.

This idea of breathing in and out, and rhythm is prevalent in the Bible. When God released the Israelites from slavery in Egypt, He didn't just remove them from the country of their oppression, He needed to give them back their humanity too. He needed to restore their soul. Because slavery strips you of your spirit and your humanity. It deprives you of your hope and it disempowers you. It makes you forget who you were created to be. And so when they got out of Egypt, He reminded them that they were children of God and taught them how to live and find rhythm.

He told them to breathe.

He told them to rest once a week. To work for six days and on the seventh day,

rest,
reconnect,
be.

God reminded them to breathe in, not just to breathe out.

He encouraged them to find rhythm.

Later God developed this idea of rhythm, not just encouraging them to rest for a day a week, but also to build in a rhythm of celebration and festivals.

A rhythm of feasting and fasting.
A rhythm of remembering and giving thanks.
A rhythm of family and community.
A rhythm of giving and generosity.
A rhythm of forgiveness and freedom.

Rhythm.

Breathing in.

Breathing out.

Rhythm.

That invitation is extended to us today. God continues to encourage us to live lives of rhythm. In a world that demands we are always busy, God invites us to rest, to breathe, to take time out and be. In a world that is so pressured and competitive, God reminds us that it is OK to be you. He loves you just as you are. He made you, He delights in you and He loves wasting time with you. And He invites you to waste time with Him.

God invites you to waste time with Him.

In a society that is so stressed and anxious, God reminds us to share His blessing with the community. To find rhythms of love, sacrifice and mercy that bring hope and peace and redemption to the world around us.

In a world that is so obsessed with more,
and money,
and image,
and status,
and possessions,

God invites us to find rhythms of generosity and to choose the path of less and simplicity.

And this isn't just true for us as individuals,

but also for us as the church.

It is important we find the rhythm of breathing as a church.

That the more we breathe out into the community, the more we need to spend time breathing in the restorative beauty of God.

We are invited to find rhythms of worship and prayer and being, alongside our habits of love, sacrifice and serving our community.

We are invited to change the world together and have fun together.

To celebrate together and to cry together.

We are invited to love God and to love others.

We are invited to be blessed and to be the blessing.

We are encouraged to find rhythms of generosity to others, and to each other.

Rhythms of forgiveness and grace.

We are invited to breathe God in.

And to breathe God out.

To breathe God in.

And breathe God out.

To breathe in.

And to breathe out.

Breathe in.

Breathe out.

And breathe.

seep

A couple of years ago, I took a sabbatical. Time to breathe. Time to go away with God and listen, waste time and breathe God in. Time to look to the future. Dream together. Laugh together. Breathe.

I would recommend it if you get the chance.

One conversation I had during my sabbatical was with Sarah, a member of my leadership team, who asked me a question that made me pause and think for a while.

She asked me,

> 'What does worship look like for you, Adam?'

It stopped me.

Such a simple question in so many ways, and yet it seemed to take me deep inside myself.

The reason she asked is because I am not an obvious worshipper. Which can be a problem for a church leader. I am more of a processor than a worshipper.

I'm more of an introvert than an extrovert, and this plays out during worship.

I am aware that it can be difficult if the church leader doesn't always appear to be consumed in worship. Not least for the worship leader. But that's me. It's not that I don't ever sing or raise my hands. I do. But not lots. I tend to be more contemplative. I tend to be sat down, sometimes with my head in my hands.

Again, not always the most encouraging sight for the worship leader.

But neither do I want to be the church leader who pretends, or sings and raises his hands when its not authentic. I don't want to be a church leader who worships just to demonstrate what worship looks like, or lead the church in to worship.

And I'm not saying that's right, its just where I'm at.

So don't be surprised if you see me sat down during worship. But also don't assume that it means I am not worshipping. God and I can go to some deep and profound places in those moments. We can have some tough conversations. I can spend time wrestling with myself and with God. I can be lost in beauty and awe, or stuck in struggle and frustration, and my appearance will be much the same.

Anyway, that's why Sarah asked me the question.

And I stopped.

I stopped because I didn't want to give a flippant answer.
I didn't want to give a self-justifying answer.

I instantly became just as intrigued by the answer as Sarah was.

What does worship look like for me?

After some considerable time and contemplation I developed an answer which made sense of me. An answer which rang true. And an answer that challenged me.

My answer was that worship looks like taking the time to allow the things I have come to understand about God in my head, to seep into my heart. Giving them the time to seep into my soul and become part of me. Allowing them to form me, so they are forged into my DNA, and change me.

You see, my mind is a busy place. It is almost constantly racing with new ideas, solutions to problems, theories, questions, paradoxes, theological inconsistencies, challenges of language, analysing myself, analysing others, critiquing theology of worship songs, finding theological threads in movies, songs, tv shows and news items, working out why Manchester United aren't winning as much as they used to, or how to respond to my child in a particular situation, or why a certain political argument appeals to so many people, or wondering why we end up looking like the things we oppose so much, and so on and so on.

My mind is a busy place.

So when I come to some new revelation of what God is like, or I stumble across some new mind-blowing revelation in scripture, or a new question in the Bible that sends me reeling, or I recognise something in my own spirituality, or I hear a great challenge in a sermon, or in a book, or in a blog, or post, or tweet, it inspires me and challenges me. It gets my mind spinning, and invariably it gets me on my feet, pacing around or wanting to work it through in a conversation or on a huge whiteboard, or on a wall somewhere.

You get the picture.

But often what I end up doing is externalising it.

What I often end up doing is sharing it with someone, or even identifying someone who needs to hear it because it just might be the thing that helps them work through a particular issue. I might even see how it might fit into a sermon that's coming up, or a piece of writing I'm working on.

In short, I see how it could be really helpful to anyone but me.

I externalise it.

I process it, recognise its relevance, or brilliance, or challenge, but then I pass it on.

Without ever giving it the time to do anything IN me.

I acknowledge it in my head.
It fits into my narrative or understanding.
It does something for me,

But I don't give it the time to do anything in me.

I don't give it the time to change me,
or form me,
or liberate me,
or transform me,
or disrupt me,
or uncover me.

I don't give it the time to seep into my soul.

I realised in that moment, that that's what worship looks like for me.
It's when I allow time for these things. These ideas, questions,
revelations, concepts or problems, to seep into me. Into my heart.
Into my soul. And give them the time to get into me and form me.

Because when I do, they colour everything. When they get into
the core of me, then they come out in all sorts of ways. Then I
can teach on them with authenticity. Then I can share them with
authority. Because they have done something in me first, and they
come from a place of experience, not just understanding.

But that sort of thing doesn't happen quickly.

And so we need to breathe.

We need to stop, pause, listen, rest.

We need to breathe in so that we can breathe out.

We need to absorb God so that we can express God.

And sometimes the hardest thing to do

is to breathe.

Sometimes the hardest thing to do

is to give God the time to seep into us and transform us.

Sometimes the hardest thing to do

is to do nothing.

Sometimes the hardest thing to do

is

to

stop.

fifth

'Honour your father and your mother, so that you may live long in the land the Lord your God is giving you.'

NIV

tuck

It's not easy being a pastor's kid. I wouldn't say it's something I enjoyed very much. There are a few reasons for this. People watch you all the time. You are expected to be perfect. You are supposed to be an example to the other children. You are punished more severely and praised less. You are the first to arrive at church and the last to leave. In fact you spend so much time at church that it can become difficult to differentiate between the church building and home. Church leaders aren't paid very well either, but they are asked to give a lot, and so the family often suffers both ways. You struggle to make ends meet, whilst seeing the church take all the time and energy your parents have. None of these are good, and they are my experience, and I suspect the experience of many other pastor's kids too. Including my own. But there are two other reasons I want to talk about some more.

The first of these is illustrated best by a story.

I remember a Bible week run at our church when I was little. We had a group of American students come over and run youth groups for us, with awesome puppet shows, crazy games, catchy songs, Bible quizzes, hilarious stories and a tuck shop.

I'm not sure to this day why we call it 'tuck' rather than sweets.

I loved this week. The American students were so cool and fun to be around. I did not know that Christians could be like that. And one of the things I loved about the week was that there was a competition. We got points for knowing our memory verses, being fastest at the Bible drills and winning Bible quizzes. And the child with the most points at the end of the week won a £5 voucher at the tuck shop, which in the 1970's was a huge amount of money to a seven year old. I remember working out that I could have bought over thirty chocolate bars.
Another thing you should probably know about me at this point in the story is that I am competitive. I don't mean competitive in that it's nice to win. I mean competitive in that I have to win. And I don't just win by trying hard, I win by working out strategies, analysing

the game to see how I can maximise my efforts, analysing my opponents to identify my biggest threats and then establishing how I can minimise their threat. I really like to win. All of which suggests that whilst I knew my Bible well, I didn't actually know my Bible at all. I knew what it said and could quote it, find it, and reference it, but I didn't quite grasp the significance of verses such as,

'the first will be last and the last will be first.'

Anyway, back to the story.

All of this to say, that when I was presented with this competition during our Bible week, I decided that I would win. I made sure that I knew every single Bible verse. I practiced my Bible drills, and was focused on the quizzes. I worked hard that week, and I won. I didn't just edge it either. I won quite comfortably as I remember. So much so that I was uncatchable by the time we got to the final day. My friends were nearly as excited as I was, because there was no way I could eat all that chocolate and all those sweets by myself.

I walked in like a king. My name was top of the score board, as it had been all week. This was my moment. This was the fruit of all the hard work. Victory was such a sweet moment. We relaxed on the final day. Lots of fun. Lots of laughter. I still knew my memory verses and I still aced the quiz, but it was all immaterial now. Then we came to the moment. The culmination of the week. I imagine the culmination of the week in the minds of the American students was the gospel message and altar call, but to me that was a distraction. The real culmination, the pinnacle, the moment we had all been working towards, was the declaration of the winner. And this was it. They introduced my Dad up on stage, as the pastor of the church, to announce the winner which was a bit frustrating because I would rather be congratulated by one of the cool students, but never mind, it was OK. I was still going to enjoy it.

But then my Dad said that whilst I had the most points, they had decided that it wouldn't be fair to give it to me, and so they had decided to give the prize to the girl who came in second place.

WHAT?

I felt like I had quite a good grasp on what was fair and not fair, and right now I was drowning in a sea of not fair. I was overwhelmed by an avalanche of not fair. How could they not give it to me?

Tears started welling up and my eyes started stinging. I fought hard to keep it together. I already had to deal with the shame of facing my friends who had all been promised chocolate bars, I couldn't handle the shame of crying. But here they came.

Tears started trickling down my cheeks and I couldn't stop them. The injustice was raw within me.

I don't know whether he could see that I was upset, but my Dad said that they 'would sort something out for me afterwards' but what good was that?
Where was my moment?
Where was my glory?
Where was my £5?

Sometimes I hated being a pastor's kid.

My Mum saw that I was upset and came to speak to me, and I told her what I thought in no uncertain terms. I told her what I thought of the competition, the Bible week, and particularly what I thought of my Dad. She reminded me that the Bible said that I should honour my parents, to which I reminded her that in Ephesians 6 it says

'fathers do not exasperate your children'.
NIV

So maybe the Bible study had been worthwhile after all.

I tell this story, because pastor's kids, or at least this pastor's kid, wasn't allowed to win anything. And for some pastor's kids that might not be an issue, but for this pastor's kid who really liked to win, it was a big issue. And it happened time and time again. And it made the command to honour your parents a real challenge for me on many an occasion.

broken

The second reason it's not easy being a pastor's kid is because your faith is entirely entwined with your family. There are many blessings to this, because you have the privilege of growing up in a Christian home, hearing about God and Jesus, being part of a community of people who love God, learning to pray and worship, and knowing your Bible. Church is generally a safe place with good people who are all trying to live out their faith, so what can go wrong with that?

But things can go wrong. And things did go wrong for me.

I should start by saying that in many ways my Dad was a good Dad and a good man. He was a great preacher and an effective church leader. But he was flawed in some ways. I am sure this is not unusual, but for me it caused some issues with my faith and my relationship with church.

One of the first times I became aware of a problem was in my early teens when I began to notice a disconnect between what my Dad said and what my Dad did. Sometimes I would be aware that he was lying about something. It would be something quite trivial usually. I am sure that many kids encounter this with their parents, but when it's the same man preaching on a Sunday, then the obvious question is, 'is he telling the truth now?'

Sometimes he would express a view about politics or football which was quite harsh or angry. And sometimes I would be aware that it wasn't true, or it seemed irrational.

There is nothing unusual in a teenager realising that there is more to the world than their parent's views or world, but for me this was entwined in my faith and religion. Which was quite complicated.

He didn't always treat my Mum well or show her the respect she deserved. He would criticise her, or tell her off for something quite petty. I began to suspect that they weren't happy or getting on very well, but on Sundays they would smile and hold hands and look like everything was perfect. But if that wasn't true, then what else wasn't true.

And then, when I was in my late teens, a bombshell hit the family. I was out at a party on a Saturday night, when my brother arrived unexpectedly to take me home.

Something had happened.

When I got home I was met by my parents who sat with us and explained that my Dad had been having an affair. The affair was over now, but the next day he was going to tell the church.

The effect of this was entirely catastrophic on so many levels.

The same day he told the church, the leaders of the church told him to leave. This meant that we all had to leave. We were each told that we weren't welcome to attend or visit the church anymore. My friends were told that they weren't allowed to invite me to events any more, or any place where church youth were gathering, which resulted in effective exile. And all this happened in twenty four hours.

I should explain here, that whilst at the time this caused huge emotional damage in me, I have since come to at least understand the church's response. My Dad was a strong leader who was actually very insecure, and so he surrounded himself with followers rather than leaders. He built the church around him. People loved him. People loved his teaching. He travelled around the world speaking, advising and counselling. He built, in many ways, a very successful church. But it was all built around him. He developed a culture where no one was able to challenge or question him. He never taught them to be leaders, just followers. He didn't raise up successors. And so when the moment came where they needed to lead through a crisis, they did the best they could with a difficult situation and a very difficult man.

The church suffered for many years afterwards in a number of ways which aren't for this book, but I believe that at least some of those issues stemmed from a failure of my Dad to equip the leaders to lead, a failure to raise up successors, and the fact that it was a church built around personality.

My Mum stayed with my Dad and tried to make it work, mainly out of a sense religious duty alongside the fact that my little sister was only aged five at this point. I think it's possibly fair to say that they understood the letter of the law, but missed the heart of the law. Whilst their marriage lasted for another twenty years or so, it never recovered. They never managed to model a healthy relationship, and ultimately my Dad had another affair. And this time he didn't come back.

It was catastrophic for me and my siblings. We were presented with a huge disconnect. Our understanding of God and church and reality was all entwined with our experience of our family. And so when our family came tumbling down, rather than our church and our faith being the things we could turn to in order to get us through, our church and our faith came tumbling down too.

At the time we needed our church the most, our church was unable to be what we needed them to be.

At a time when we needed to be able to refer to a model of faith and how faith in God can get you through a crisis, our pastor was more broken than we were. And worse still, he was the cause of the crisis, rather than the inspiration through the crisis.

I didn't really go to church for a while after that. I needed space. I needed to work life out a bit. And Christians weren't top of my list of people I wanted to be around. I didn't go to university, possibly to prove some sort of point to my Dad, because he was very keen that I should. Instead I got a job as a waiter in Manchester and found a new community. And this was a beautiful thing. I worked out my faith in a new way. Not in a church but with a broad and diverse community of people, from all walks of life, with all sorts of experiences. All backgrounds, all ages, all classes, all sexualities, all genders, all nationalities, all races and ethnicities. All faiths and mainly none. I worked out my faith. I worked out my relationship with God. I went to church a little when I could, a church that gave me space to be. A space to ask questions. A space to doubt. A space to heal. But much of my healing and acceptance and love came from my community in Manchester city centre. It came in the bars and the restaurants. Amongst the drunk people and the addicts. The families and couples. The sports stars and the rock stars. The gay clubs and the jazz clubs. The bouncers and the chefs and the bartenders and the waitresses.

These were my people, and God was with me and with them. In me and in them. And we laughed together and cried together and argued together and danced together and partied together and shared life together. And they didn't mind that I didn't drink or do drugs or sleep around or fight or swear or whatever else.

I look back on those times with fond memories of beautiful people and crazy moments and long weekends, and I see God with me. I see God holding me and finding me. I see God shaping me and healing me.

And then, sat on my bed one day, God spoke to me. It wasn't a loud voice, just one of those times when something hits you and there's no getting away from it. It isn't just an idea, it's from the deepest part of you. I know it was God because there was no way this was me.

God wanted me to go to Bible college.

I didn't really like being around Christians for one day a week, and now God was asking me to live with them seven days a week.

I was horrified.

I resisted it quite strongly, but there was no escaping that this was what I was supposed to do. And so I negotiated. I told God that if this is what He wanted, then I would only go to a particular Bible college. It was in England, only an hour away from home so I could always escape if I needed to, and it needed to be this year.

I thought this would be a problem because they probably wouldn't have a place and I didn't have any money to pay for it, so there was no way this was going to work out.

I called the Bible college up and got through to the director, who knew my Dad quite well. We talked for a while and then I dropped it on him that I thought I should be going to college this year.

His response floored me.

He said that they are normally full by this point in the year, however they had sensed God telling them to reserve a place for someone who would apply late. They also said that I should pay what I can, but it was more important that I came, so not to worry about the funding.

Floored.

So I went, living with one hundred and sixty Christians from all over the world for seven months.

And it was incredible.

I was able to explore my faith and work out what I believed and what I didn't. I was able to pray and listen and bless and be blessed. I made deep friendships and a deep connection with God. And whilst I was there God spoke to me again, telling me that one day, I would lead a church.

My response to this was of the Jonah variety. I promised God that I would do anything He wanted, go anywhere He wanted, serve in any way He wanted, but I would not lead a church. The pain of church was still very deep, and God knew that, and so He gave me a lot of time.

Ten years in fact.

And ten years later, when I was thirty one, God reminded me of who He had called me to be and I became a youth leader. Still against my will somewhat. Still kicking and screaming somewhat. But we settled on a job as youth leader of a church in the south west of England, in a town called Yeovil, which I had to look up on a map.

I grew to love my role as youth leader, and particularly the young people I was serving. I even got used to being totally immersed in a church community again, but I wasn't ready for it when, five years later, I was asked to lead the church.

redeem

I was sat in a ski chalet in the Alps and it was 9am. I was on retreat to breathe, and pray and dream about where next for the youth and the community projects I was leading. It was day one and I opened my Bible. As I did, a piece of paper fell out. On the paper were some notes from a message given to the church a couple of years earlier. It talked of a new time, when the church would be a blessing to the whole community. Reflect Jesus in the world. Be a voice for the voiceless. You get the sort of idea.

But this time, as I read this for what felt like the first time, I had that clear sense of God speaking to me again. This time telling me that when I returned, I would be the guy to lead the church into this new time.

Floored.

Again.

We had a really great leader, who wasn't talking about leaving. A leader who inspired me and taught me. Why would he leave? And why would anyone think that I should take the church on? I'm an ideas person. I'm a creative. I'm a visionary. I'm an activist. And if I know anything about churches, I know that activists and creatives don't get asked to lead churches. I'm far too risky. And, as we have discussed previously, I didn't really want the gig.

I decided to say nothing.

If it was God, then God would make it happen.

The week after I got back from my retreat, my leader took me away for a day to meet his mentor. We sat in the room together and got straight to the point. They both felt that it was the right time for me to take on leading the church.

And totally floored again.

Then they both looked at me and asked me for my thoughts, and I told them about what had happened in the Alps.

But this is where it gets beautiful. My leader said that he would step down in nine months after taking the church through the transition process. He also said that he would seek to get the whole leadership team to offer to step down so I could choose my own leadership team.

Have you ever heard anything like that?

So I had nine months to hear God. Nine months to explore the vision, to decide on a team, to look at different models of church, and to understand who God was calling me to be.

And this is why I tell this story here, in relation to this command.

Because what does it look like to follow in the steps of your father when your father has been so gifted in so many ways, and yet made so many mistakes?

What does it look like to recognise the gifting and calling you have inherited, along with the pitfalls and flaws?

What does it look like to step into a role that carries so much pain, and sadness for you, alongside so much calling and identity?

How do I honour my parents in this situation?

And so God and I talked about some principles.

We talked about principles of who He created me to be.
We talked about humility and wisdom.
We talked about submission and obedience.
We talked about the problems of power and control.
We talked about forgiveness and healing,
We talked about giving space for others.
We talked about diversity and vulnerability.

And I chose a team. I chose a team because I didn't want the pitfalls of being a leader on my own, and so I chose a team that would work with me, and hold me accountable. I chose a team that was diverse. Diverse in age, experience, gender, and theology. I actively chose people who are different to me. People who think differently. People who disagree with me on things. Because I came to understand that I need to have strong people around me.

People who will lead. People who will challenge. People who are loyal and love me and are for me, but people who aren't intimidated by me or fear me. We need a team of different voices so we can see as much of the picture as possible. Each person bringing their piece of the picture and submitting it to the bigger picture. Not a group of people who want to win, or need to impose their view. And that includes me. We need a team of different voices who can discern God's will together. We need different voices so we can lead and reflect a diverse church.

Different voices matter.

And when we have a diverse team, then I as leader, submit to that team. I came to understand that it is a failure of leadership to impose my view. It is a failure of leadership to use my title. And so I lead the team as a member of the team. with one voice amongst many. Even as a visionary leader, it was important for me to understand how to use that gifting. Rather than being a leader with a big idea who is able to get other people to follow, I came to see my role as someone who hears everyone's hopes and dreams and vision. Everyone's ideas. And then, as the visionary leader, my role is to distil those dreams and hopes and visions down into language and ideas that encapsulate a sense of everyone's passion. So everyone can look at our vision and get behind it, because their dreams are part of it. Their identity is embedded in it.

I become a facilitator of vision, rather than an imposer of vision.

We talked about ways to avoid me becoming the personality the church is built around. And so I try not to be the guy. We ensure that my voice is just one voice of many. I don't do all the teaching. I don't do all the communicating. We have a range of voices and styles. We make space for people. We make space for others. I tend not to get involved in pastoral situations. There are some exceptions, but these are primarily dealt with by small group leaders, or other members of the leadership team.

All to avoid the problems of personality-led church.

And then I have a group of people who I meet with every week, to talk about the heart of who we are as a church. A place where I can have accountability. A place where we work out life and God and leadership together. And the leadership team is a place where we pray for each other and the church. A place where we hear God together. A place where I am allowed to be me. A place where I am allowed to not be OK. A place where we get to be real.

Because this is how I honour my parents.

I don't hide from my gifting. I don't hide from my heritage. But I learn from it. I don't hide from the story I am part of, or the story I am invited to continue to work out. I celebrate who I am and what I inherited. I recognise who my Dad was called to be. I recognise who God was in him, but I also see what he allowed to get in the way. I see the things that derailed him. I see the things that he got wrong and made him come up short. And now, every day, I have an opportunity to repeat those mistakes or redeem them. I have an opportunity to repeat the patterns or redeem them.

Repeat or redeem.

I recognise and honour the story I am part of. I pick out the threads and patterns of beauty and gifting that I inherit from my parents, and their parents, and their parents before them. And I take those threads and patterns, I take that DNA, and I carry on the story. I continue to work it out, bringing colour and depth and vibrancy to them.

But I don't just honour the good,
I have an opportunity to redeem the broken and the bad too.

I don't have to repeat the destructive cycles, or the paths of addiction or disconnection. I have an opportunity to redeem. I have a choice to repeat the behaviour or redeem it. I can lead in the same ways, or I can forge new paths. I can bring some of the destructive attitudes or behaviours into my marriage that did so much damage to my parents marriage, or I can choose new paths. I can choose paths of redemption. I can choose paths that break the destructive cycles and redeem them.

Repeat or redeem.

It's a choice I get to make every day.

Do I allow my weaknesses, or those I saw in my Dad's story to distract me or derail me? Do I allow myself to resort to power or control. To seek identity or affirmation from people. To allow my insecurity to dictate my behaviour and my words, or do I submit to who God created me to be. Do I allow God to have His way and to work out paths of hope and love and restoration and humility and beauty and redemption.

This is why the command says that if we honour our parents it will result in us living well in the land God has given us. Because we are part of a bigger story. One that goes on from generation to generation, and our purpose is to take the good, and the holy and the beautiful and the life-giving and the gifting that we inherit, and build on it.

To continue the story and pass it on to the next generation.

To expand the patterns and rhythms of life and beauty and hope and generosity, and encourage them in the next generation. To build on the gifting that is in our DNA and take steps towards it being realised. Take steps towards it being fulfilled, so we can pass it on to our kids in better shape than we inherited it.

And where we inherit patterns and rhythms that are destructive and shrink us and distort us, then we have an opportunity to break those cycles so our children don't have to. We have an opportunity to redeem them and establish new, life-giving patterns that will bless our children rather than being a curse or a burden to them.

Every day is an opportunity to build on the successes.

Every day is an opportunity to break the destructive cycles.

Every day is an opportunity to repeat or redeem.

Every day is an opportunity to honour my parents.

sixth

'You shall not murder.'
NIV

kill

It just so happens that I am writing this chapter on a Tuesday towards the end of May in 2017. Last night, in my home city of Manchester, a terrorist attacked an Ariana Grande concert in the city. It was a concert filled with 20,000 people. Many of them young children. Many going to their first concert. All having fun, listening and singing along to music they love. Seeing their favourite singer for the first time perhaps.

A really special, beautiful night of celebration and life.

And then, as the concert ended, with parents waiting for their children outside, a man detonated a bomb.

Panic.

Death.

Fear.

Separation.

Loss.

A truly horrific event in the history of a great city.
A truly horrific event in the history of a nation, a continent, and a world.
An act of death.
An act of hate.
An act designed to destroy, kill, divide and shrink us.

I was watching TV at the time, when an alert popped up on Twitter. We turned over to watch the news. We contacted my niece who had been in the city centre that night, indeed, had been right by the arena just a few hours earlier. We wanted to know she was safe.

And then we sat, tears in our eyes, as we watched the situation unfold before us.

Chaos.

Confusion.

Fear

Trauma.

Families separated.

Parents helpless.

Children crying.

News presenters breaking down in tears as they listen to stories of parents desperate for news of children who haven't come home.

People searching the hospitals and hotels for partners or children or parents.

Reporters working hard to piece together snippets of information amid rumours and confusion.

Reports of bodies on the ground. Children lost. Parents desperate. Fleets of ambulances rushing to the scene. Hundreds of police officers running into the building. Injuries. Death. Suffering. Hate. Terrorism.

And then, within minutes, stories of hope.

#roomformanchester started trending on Twitter, as people all over Manchester offered a bed to anyone in need and unable to get home or to their hotel.

Taxi drivers turned their metres off and drove people anywhere they needed to go.

People coming out of their homes with drinks and food for anyone who needed it.

People on Twitter offering to drive people anywhere, bring money, clothes or blankets to anyone who needed them.

Hotels taking in children who had been separated from their parents, giving them a safe place to wait and be reconnected.

Hotels giving away all their spare rooms free and restaurants opening their doors.

Manchester responded with courage, and generosity and love.

Extraordinary.

Inspiring stories of kindness and selflessness.

All within a matter of minutes of the explosion.

Manchester's instinctive response was one of generosity, kindness and love.

Manchester's instinctive reaction was to pull together, and stand together as a community.

To choose love over hate.

To choose to expand rather than shrink in the face of adversity and fear.

To choose generosity and kindness in the face of evil and death.

Manchester showed something of what God is like last night and it's partly why I am still crying this morning.

Amidst the deep sadness and shock and tears of seeing my city suffer, families ripped apart, and people killed brutally, I also see hope and beauty and kindness.
And hope gets to me, especially in the darkest moments.

Hope amidst pain is a powerful thing.
Beauty amidst ashes is a profound thing.
Kindness and love amidst death and hate does something in us that is hard to describe.

The sixth command is 'you shall not murder', and in many ways I imagine it requires the least explanation. Death is so destructive. Murder is so devastating for so many people. The finality of it. The suddenness of it. The trauma and pain and loss and horror of it. It's hard to imagine. The impact is so profound and so far-reaching.

That God, the creator of life, should condemn murder is no surprise. God is the God who breathes life into us. Jesus declared Himself to be 'The Way, The Truth and The Life'. God is the creator of life, and invites us to be creators of life too. He invites us to be people of life too. In Deuteronomy 30, God presents His people with the choice between blessing and curses, life and death, and then implores them to choose life.

Life matters.

It is who God is. In the gospels, when Jesus encountered people who had died, invariably they came back to life. Because God isn't a God of death, He is a God of life. We don't die when we encounter God, we are revived.
We are reborn.
We are renewed.
Because that is what God is like.

Life matters.

It is who God invites us to be; people who create and bring life, and beauty and hope into the world. People of generosity and kindness. People who heal and restore and renew and transform. People who forgive and love.

And so when we murder, we act in opposition to our God given identity. We leave God's name bereft and empty. We become people of destruction and death and hate and anger and revenge and ugliness and division and pain.

We shrink.
We dehumanise.

Life matters.

And so murder is the ultimate dehumanisation.

We steal life.
We destroy life.

And not just the life we took.

Murder has a devastating effect on all the lives connected to that life. The families, the friends and the communities. We destroy and we dehumanise. We rip families and communities apart. So often, we see families that have suffered the death of a child becoming deeply fractured and broken, often developing issues around mental health, divorce, addiction, and more.

Grief can sit in us and overwhelm us and rob whole families of futures and memories and joy and life.

And murder affects the murderer too.

Not just if they suffer the legal or social consequences, but within themselves too. We aren't created to take life, we are created to give life. And so when we act violently in opposition to this it can distort us and damage us.

So God instructs us not to kill.

Because that's not what we are created for.

Instead He invites us to be people of life. People of blessing. When we encounter death and hate and murder and fear and destruction and violence, like we did in Manchester last night, we are presented with a choice.

Will we react to hate with hate?
violence with violence?
death with death?

Or will we be people of life?

Will we be people of hope who respond with love and kindness
and generosity?

Will we be people who expand rather than shrink?

People who bless rather than curse?

People who stand up and reflect something of what God is like?

And so this morning, amidst my tears,

I choose love.

I choose hope.

I choose life.

seventh

'You shall not commit adultery.'
NIV

necklace

I am sure that you, like everyone, have various Christmas traditions.
In our family we are no different. One of ours is to go on a drive
around the town looking at all the Christmas lights people have
put up.
One of those traditions, like nearly all families, involves Christmas
films. Every Christmas has to include time to watch a range of
films, and we all have our own favourites. We all love Elf and it is
usually watched more than once. Home Alone and Home Alone 2
are firm favourites too.

Rachel and I will always watch It's a Wonderful Life, and at least
some of us will watch Miracle on 34th Street. The whole family
loves Nativity, which if you haven't seen it, is a film about a school
teacher trying to put on the school nativity and trying to convince
'Hollywood' to come over and film it. Its better than it sounds and I
would highly recommend it.

But another of our favourites is Love Actually. It's a film with a range
of story lines around love and relationships, all based around the
Christmas period, and all interlinked in a variety of ways. It is a
lovely, hope-filled movie, with some really pain-filled storylines.

One of these involves a couple played by Alan Rickman and Emma
Thompson. They are married, with children, and seem to have quite
a good relationship, if not a little in a rut, except he is being pursued
by his PA. She is young and pretty and blatantly flirtatious with him,
leaving him in no doubt that she is there for him is he wants her.
As he is heading out one day to do some Christmas shopping with
his wife, his PA asks him if he is planning to buy her a present. He
pauses and asks her what she needs. Does she need something
for the office? But she replies saying,

I don't want something I need, I want something I want.'

Whilst his wife is off in another department of the store, he sees a
gold necklace and decides to buy it for his PA. This leads to a

hilarious scene where Rowan Atkinson plays a fastidious sales assistant who insists on taking an age to wrap this gift in the most extravagant way, much to Alan Rickman's frustration. Nevertheless, the necklace ends up being bought, and when at home, his wife finds it in his coat pocket, and whilst a little stunned, is excited that he should have bought her such a beautiful gift.

Fast forward to Christmas Eve, and the family are opening one present each before going to the school Christmas performance. Emma Thompson picks out the present she thinks is the necklace and opens it, only to reveal a CD of Joni Mitchell.

The necklace was not for her after all.

She absents herself to the bedroom for a while, and we see this stunning scene of pain, and loss, and betrayal and devastation, all without saying a word, as she sits on her bed, her world falling apart around her, as she comes to term with the fact that the necklace wasn't for her. It was for someone else. She plays the role brilliantly, and it is harrowing to watch, because she makes you feel her pain. A little later, at the school performance, she grabs a moment with her husband, and asks him, 'What would you do if you were in my situation? Would you wait around to find out if it was just a necklace, or sex and a necklace, or even worse, love?'

What a devastating question to be asked.
What a devastating question to have to ask.

But all of this brings us to a big question about the command on adultery. Because we don't know whether the character has committed adultery or not, we only know he has given his PA a necklace in response to her sexual advances. We don't know if he has gone any further.

But what is apparent is that it is almost irrelevant.

The damage of the necklace is just as significant. The devastation and betrayal his wife feels at the necklace is enormous, and justifiably so. It has ripped the family apart. Emma Thompson's character says that she now knows that life will never be the same again. The repercussions of this act, this gift, are life long and catastrophic. The deep betrayal and disconnection may never be overcome, and may even be too much for the marriage to bear.

But he hasn't even broken any command.

We don't know that he has committed adultery.

He just bought a necklace.

And the Ten Commandments don't say anything about that. By the law, he is still OK with God, he hasn't done anything wrong.

But his actions have caused huge disconnection and pain.

The law is inadequate.

It would not be OK for him to point to the law and declare himself innocent, because that would be entirely missing the point.

All of which suggests that the law as a legal framework of what is acceptable to God and what is not, seems to fall short.

So is the law ineffective at defining who is good enough?

What if the law is ineffective as a measure of sin?

What if sin is about more than just breaking a rule, or a list of rules?

What if sin isn't about breaking rules at all?

sex

I am sure all of us who have ever been a youth leader, or a church leader, or a Sunday school teacher have had one of those moments. You know, when something happens you were just not prepared for and it changes everything you were about to do, or about to say, or even challenges some of your theology which you thought you were pretty certain on. And however thought through and planned your session was, or your sermon was, or your talk was, you come to this sudden realisation that you hadn't planned this well at all. Something happens which throws you a real curveball and you are the one left changed and a little shaken.

Well this was one of those moments, and you will be delighted to know, it involved the Ten Commandments.

We run a large youth project which brings in young people aged between 18-25 from all over the world, and we disciple them, teach them youth work and engage them in the schools, run drop in sessions in the community, do detached youth work in the parks and on the streets, play football, skating, dance classes and a whole lot more stuff. It's like a gap year programme, although now its evolved into a more creative programme around music and media, alongside the other stuff and also students can stay for up to four years and get degrees in theology alongside youth work or children and families' work or even missional leadership. It's a really great programme.

Anyway, this programme meant that we were engaging with a wide range of youth, from church kids through to kids from across the community who had no connection with church at all. Not for generations in some cases. It was beautiful to see the challenges and connections when they mixed together.

Everyone was changed.This wasn't a programme to get the non church kids looking like the church ones. This wasn't so much an exercise in evangelism, as it was an exercise in community. It was an exercise in connection and love. This was a programme where we invited the church kids along with us to hang out with the others, so that we would all be changed. We would find God in each other.

It is worth mentioning here, that even now, as leader of the church, we run and are involved in a large number of projects in the community, from family support, to job clubs, to food banks, to counselling, to debt crisis management, to street pastors, to parent and toddler groups, to the night shelter, and the list goes on and on.

But we don't run these programmes to get the community into the church, we run them to get the church into the community, so that as we encounter and share life with the family in crisis, or the homeless, or the addict, or the unemployed, or the sick, or the desperate, we are all changed by the encounter. We see God in the eyes of the hopeless and hurting and hungry. We are connected to them and we share the journey with them, and invite them to share the journey with us. It is not a work of charity, it is a work of love, and compassion and justice.

It is kingdom in action.

We stand alongside. We align ourselves with the others and the outsiders. We help those without a voice to find their voice. We empower people to make choices that change their situation. We invite people into a journey of transformation. We invite people into a new future. One that isn't defined by their past. And as we do this, we are changed too. We are transformed too. We discover a new future too.

Anyway, back to the story.

So we're running a youth alpha session, and the subject is sin. And so I had planned to do a little exercise based around the Ten Commandments. Everyone would be stood up, and I would call out various of the Ten Commandments, and if you had broken that command you would sit down. The point of the exercise was to demonstrate in a light-hearted way that we had all sinned, which would lead me into a conversation about what sin was, and whether how we understood sin might change how we viewed God and ourselves and our situation.

Which should give you a heads up about where we are headed.

Anyway, I thought I would start with some of the commands that no-one had broken first and then head towards lying as my last one, feeling pretty sure that there would be no-one left standing at that point.

I started with idols, and asked if anyone had any carved images of gods in their bedroom or in their house, that they worshipped each night before they went to bed. Thankfully no one sat down and we continued. Then I asked if anyone had murdered anyone, and again, thankfully, no one sat down. Then I asked if anyone had committed adultery. Another safe one for sure, as none of them were married.

At that point one of the girls asked what adultery meant, and before I could work out how to answer, unhelpfully someone else answered it for me.

'It's when you have sex with someone you're not married to'.

Which is not the most accurate definition for the context we were in, or the point of the exercise I was doing, but there it was. It was out there, and there was no putting the cat back in the bag because instantly two or three of the girls sat down. It was a bit awkward for me, but they didn't seem phased at all. It seemed like the most natural thing for them. Which meant that they were surprised that no one else was sitting down, so one of them asked a question. She wanted to know why the Bible said this was wrong.

And that was it. That was the moment that it hit me like a freight train.

I had grown up believing that God was angry with the whole world because we were wilfully disobeying Him. I had read the Bible to say that those of us who loved God, had asked for forgiveness and now obeyed the commands were the ones He loved, and everyone else was wilfully disobeying Him. Everyone else was consciously rebelling against God and His law. People knew what was right, but were choosing to live in opposition to it because they were rebellious and so deserved their punishment of hell.

Even though my theology had moved quite considerably in many ways, I now recognised that some of the framework of that thinking remained. Whilst I no longer believed that God only loved those who loved Him, I had still somehow held onto the idea that people were consciously rebelling against God. Even though I had a different understanding of sin, which we will come on to. I still somehow believed that everyone knew what they were doing was wrong because it was obvious.

But here were two girls who had no idea that they were doing anything wrong. And they were doing the Alpha Course because they had chosen a relationship with God a few weeks earlier. They weren't trying to sin, they were trying to live life well. They were trying to do what was right. They just didn't know that having sex in their circumstance might be a problem.

Which led me to a couple of questions.

Was God really the sort of God that would punish people who weren't wilfully being bad, but were just doing the best they could, following the culture, their parents, their peers, and what they thought was expected of them?
If sin was breaking a rule, what if you didn't know about the rule? Were you still culpable for breaking it?

Which led me to another question.

Was it wrong to steal or lie, or murder, or commit adultery or any of those things, before God wrote them down on stone tablets? And if it was, why did God need to write it down?
And if it wasn't writing it down as rules that made it wrong, then what was it that made it wrong?

And so everything I thought I knew about sin and sinners was suddenly up in the air.
Everything needed re-thinking.
What if some people weren't trying to be bad?
What if most people were actually trying to make good decisions? And if we were trying to make good decisions, why did we end up in such a mess?
And how did this fit in with how I understood sin?

disconnect

Sin was central to the Gospel I grew up with.

Sin was disobedience, or rebellion, or breaking the rules.

The result of this was that we were disconnected from God.

I remember being presented with a diagram where God was on one side of a canyon and I was on the other and the word 'SIN' was written in the space of the canyon. My sin meant that God and I were separated. The consequence of this sin and separation was that I would die, and would be separated from God for eternity. This is because God can not have anything to do with sin because He is holy, and so I am unacceptable to God.

It's a bit like the mountain I talked about. God is angry with me at the top, and I am at the bottom ashamed. Not good enough. Sinful.

I am unacceptable to God and God is inaccessible to me.

However, there is hope.

Jesus died on the cross, sinless, taking the punishment of death for my sin. And so the diagram shows the cavern being filled now by a cross, which acts as a bridge across to God, so we can be reunited, and I can spend eternity in relationship with Him. If I accept this sacrifice, and commit my life to God, I am forgiven of all my sin, and I can be assured of my place in heaven.

This Gospel presents some issues though.

Firstly, it can result in us seeing the main point of our salvation as being about going to heaven, rather than a more expansive view of what it is to live with God in relationship now, here on earth.

This can result in us seeing our salvation as the end of the story, rather than the beginning.

We can end up holding on to our salvation, and protecting it, rather than learning how to live it out and work it out.

Secondly, it can become quite an individualistic gospel. Jesus died for me, so that I can have relationship with God and I can go to heaven when I die. I have even heard people say

'If you were the last person on earth, Jesus would have still died for you.'

So I become the focal point of my salvation. I become the end game of Jesus' death and resurrection. It becomes all about me.

Thirdly, it can become quite a small gospel, about quite a small god. It can diminish my ideas of who God is, who I am, what sin is, and what salvation looks like.

But I think the story is much bigger than that.

In Genesis, we see this story about our relationship with God and the impact of sin. The writers paint a picture of God as relational. Rather than a story of gods at war with each other, and a story of violence, like we see in the Babylonian creation story, we see God in relationship with Himself.

Interdependent,
interconnected,
loving relationship.

And God creates.

As God speaks, God creates.

Creation is an expression of who God is. His words call out life and beauty and creation. And then God says,

'let us make man in our image' .

Let's make man as a visible representation of what GOD, the invisible God, is like.

The writers paint a picture of God in relationship with Himself, with man and woman, and with creation. God walks with man and woman in the garden.

A beautiful picture of relationship and connectedness.

A picture of love and intimacy.

And God invites man to create and nurture. To love and be in community. To be generous and to be a blessing.

A profound and beautiful connection between God and man, man and woman, and man and creation.

This is the picture we are given of who God is, and who we are called to be. A deep connectedness. A profound knowing of each other. Unconditional, selfless love. Nothing hidden. No shame. Humanity revealing God's generous, beautiful nature to all creation. Administering God's authority and kingdom to all the earth. An act of love and submission, revealing a God of life and love.

But, as we saw earlier, the writers tell a story of overwhelming disconnection. A lie is spoken and Adam and Eve believe it. Their understanding of who God is and who they are is distorted and corrupted. They no longer want to be like God, as image bearers of the creator, but instead they want to *be* God with His knowledge and power, is the driver that leads them to rebellion. And the consequences of this rebellion are devastating and far-reaching.

We are told of the disconnection between them and God, when God is looking for them in the garden, and they are hiding. They no longer want to be in the presence of God, because of shame and fear. This is a comment on the human condition. People who are disconnected from God. Avoiding His presence because of shame and fear. Disconnected from our source of life and creativity and love and security and identity and status and purpose.

Hiding. Fearful. Ashamed. Disconnected.

But the disconnection goes further. They are also profoundly disconnected in the core of their being. Their identity is destroyed. They cover themselves. hide themselves, and mask themselves. They have lost sight of who they are, and who they were created to be. So much so that when God asks Adam why he is hiding, Adam responds by deflecting and blaming.

'That woman that you made, she ate of the apple, and gave it to me'.

In other words,

'It's your fault because you made her, and it's her fault because she made me do it.'

When we feel ashamed, when we feel exposed, we often deflect and blame, because we don't like what we see when we look at ourselves. Our shame wants to make us hide and protect, because we don't know who we are, our identity is lost, and so we deflect and accuse and blame and mock and belittle and point at others. We externalise our pain. We pretend everything is fine with us, while accusing and diminishing the other, or blaming God, or fate, or the universe, or whoever else we can blame.

This leads to another devastating disconnection. A disconnection between man and woman. A disconnection between each other. Between us. Adam blames Eve, which demonstrates a breakdown of relationship and trust. It signifies a shift to power. Where this relationship had been about love and blessing and submission to one another, preferring one another and being deeply connected to each other, now it is about blame and power and resentment. We see a deep disconnection between them, which is further emphasised when God speaks to Eve a little later in the chapter.

"I will sharpen the pain of your pregnancy,
and in pain you will give birth.
And you will desire to control your husband,
but he will rule over you."
NIV

Now, the process of life and creation they were created for and invited into, will involve suffering and pain. God also says that their relationships will be about power now. You will desire to control him and he will rule over you.

Power and control come front and centre in how we relate with each other.

It's worth mentioning here that this is a consequence of their actions that God is outlining for them here. It is not a plan B where God has decided that it's best now if man has authority over women. I have heard this passage used to demonstrate God's desire that men should rule over women and I see that as a significant distortion of the text.

Neither is it a concocted punishment by God, I.e. God has thought about the best way to punish humanity and the best punishment he can think of is to give men power over women. That would look like a spiteful and mean God.

Instead, this is a consequence of the actions. Because when we become disconnected from each other, we see each other as competition, or a threat, and so we try and assert our power over the other.

And so our relationships become about power and control rather than love and submission.

They become about strength and manipulation rather than serving and preferring.

And so we belittle and oppress and control and overcome, and kill and dehumanise and compete against each other. We try to get one over, get a step ahead, get the upper hand, get revenge, get our own back, get even and get the lion's share.

We try to get and collect, and consume, when what we are created to do is to give.

Give ground, give back, give the benefit of the doubt, give away, give ourselves, give grace, and for**give**.

But our disconnectedness, leads to relationships of power and control. In families, friendships, relationships, communities, tribes, nations, business, sport, religion, language and sex.

Everyone and everything can become competition. We end up seeing each other as threats, or someone to be bettered, beaten, overcome, overthrown, or used for my own ends or benefit.

We see people as a resource or an opportunity or an obstacle.

Which is how we can also come to see all creation. Something to be used, or abused. Something to profit from or possess or control. A source of power or strength or wealth.

And this is the fourth disconnection we see in the story in Genesis. Ultimately Adam and Eve are disconnected from creation. God warns them that they will struggle with creation. They will have to work hard and suffer.

And they are exiled from the garden.

This place of relationship, peace, unity with God, each other and creation. A place of plenty and provision and enough. A place of freedom and life and beauty.

They, and we, are disconnected from it. In all its senses.

Disconnected from God as the source of life and love and identity and relationship and security.

Disconnected within ourselves. Ashamed and afraid. Putting on masks. Learning to pretend and hide. Lost and confused. Trying to discover who we are.

Disconnected from each other, now working out our relationships in the context of power and control and competition.

And disconnected from creation. At odds with the world around us.

Quite the story.

A devastating, all-encompassing story of disconnection and loss.

A story that is continually being told throughout history, and a story which we see continuing to be told today.

All around us. In every sphere of life, in every community, in every nation, on every continent. We see this tide of disconnection rolling through history,

Which brings us back to the topic in hand.

Sin.

What if sin isn't just about disconnection from God
because we broke the rules?

What if sin is about more than a legal framework?

What if sin is about disconnection in all its forms?

What if sin isn't about the rules at all?

What if sin isn't just about disconnection from God because we broke the rules?

What if sin is about more than a legal framework?

What if sin is about disconnection in all its forms?

What if sin isn't about the rules at all?

What if sin is about all the ways in which we are disconnected and dehumanised and broken and less?

What if sin isn't about breaking some rules, but instead is about all the things we have done, and the things which have been done to us which damage us and make us less than we were created to be?

Words that are said about us, or that we have said about ourselves which play in our head telling us that we aren't enough, that we will never make it, that we aren't loved or lovable, or successful or worthwhile.

What if sin is about all the times we have used our words to hurt or damage or belittle someone, rather than to encourage or love or heal or build up?

What if sin is about thoughts we have, which become actions which become habits, which get into the core of us and distort us and twist us?

What if sin is about things that are done to us, experiences we have, that get into our souls and trap us in cycles of behaviour that hold us back and tear us down?

What if sin is about the society and the system we live in, which teaches us to hate or dismiss or ignore people? A system that tells us that some people are worth more than others. That some people don't matter. That some people don't count. A system that traps people in cycles of poverty and failure.

What if sin is about a society that always tells you that you aren't enough, and you don't have enough?

A system that always leaves you needing more and loving less.

A system that traps you in dissatisfaction and discontentment.

A system that tells you that this is how it is and this is all there is.

A system that tells you that there's no hope.

A system that teaches you violence and enmity.

A system that teaches you to use power and control to promote yourself at the expense of others.

What if sin isn't something God curses us with, but something God wants to save us from?

What if God isn't angry and disappointed, or vindictive and violent, or cruel and temperamental at all?

What if sin is about all the ways we have become less than we were created to be? Less human than our creator had in mind? Less than the potential and beauty and capacity to love and heal and bless and create that is born within us?

What if sin is about that?

And what if sin isn't the end of the story?

What if it's just the beginning?

What if we realise that all this happens in the first three chapters of the first book of a very big collection of books called the Bible?

What if we realise that this is just the first act of a very big story?

forgive

When we see the creation story in this bigger sense, then we move sin from the concept to the tangible.

As this catastrophic disconnection is realised in every aspect of ourselves, then sin moves from an idea to reality.

From some broken rules made by a distant God, to a profound loss of identity. The fracture of every relationship we know. The struggle with all creation. The loneliness that consumes our deepest thoughts. The struggle we see all around us. The system that we live in. The flaw in the DNA of society. The broken systems.

All of this is captured in the story told by the writers of the Bible thousands of years ago. They talk about a God who creates, and is in relationship. A God who invites us to create, to love, to live in freedom, to be known and to know. A God who is generous and expansive, and invites us into expansive lives of generosity. But it also tells this story of devastating disconnection.

The rest of the Bible is the story of God restoring this brokenness.

The remaining 65.94 books of the Bible, 1,186 chapters, tell the story of how God pursues us, reaches out to us, reconnects with us, loves us, and moves us towards the restoration of all things.

Everything.

Restored. Renewed. Reconnected. Redeemed.

Everything.

The realms of heaven and earth, which we see being ripped apart so dramatically in Genesis 3, are, from that point on, being pulled back together again, so by the end of revelation, we see heaven and earth restored.

The city of God being established on earth.

The realms reunited. Restored. Renewed.

We see every knee bow and every tongue speak out that Jesus is Lord.

Every single one.

Not out of duress, or fear, or force, but out of revelation. Out of love. Out of freedom. Out of restoration. Out of recognition and truth. As our only possible response to the full revelation of who God is. As our only possible response to the fullness of His beauty and glory and love.

Every single knee.

Every single voice.

Heard.

Known.

This is the trajectory of scripture.
This is the trajectory of the universe.
A trajectory of justice and love.
A trajectory of restoration and reconnection.

The prophets talk about this in a beautiful way. They talk of a time when all creation will be at peace. A time when our weapons of war and destruction will be repurposed as tools of creation and life. A time when God will be with his creation. Heaven and earth fully integrated. Fully restored. Fully renewed. A time when we will all know who God is and who we really are. A time when the systems of power and control and poverty and oppression will be over. A time when we will see everything as it truly is. God, creation, and each other. Even ourselves.

This is the trajectory of scripture. A beautiful trajectory of hope. A trajectory of forgiveness.
And forgiveness is an underrated idea.

I think this is true in society, and I think this is true in the church. In a society where revenge and getting our own back can shape our ideas of justice, forgiveness can sometimes seem like weakness, or letting somebody off the hook. In a society which is forged by the principles of competition and power, forgiveness can seem quite alien, or even foolish. And yet every now and again a story can break into the news about someone who has suffered a huge loss or injustice, and yet they talk about forgiveness, and loving their oppressor, or the person who wronged them.

It's almost like society is stopped in its tracks for a moment.

This thing that looks and sounds like weakness jars us because there is something about it that is so attractive. It's so radical. There is something about it that speaks of a different kind of strength or power. There is something of freedom about it. A love that doesn't love for gain or profit, but instead is generous, even foolish. But it stops us. It shakes us for a moment.

Forgiveness is a powerful thing when done well.

In the church, we have a problem with forgiveness too. We talk about forgiveness a lot. We confess our sins, the things we have done wrong, the rules we have broken, even our sin from birth. And we teach that God forgives us, so we can be assured of our relationship and our eternal destiny. But so often it seems like the forgiveness we talk of really kicks in when we die. It guarantees our place in heaven. It deals with God's anger with us, His hatred of our sin and His judgement.

But when we look at sin and forgiveness like this, it can lead to us missing the point.

It can mean that we fail to live in the fullness of God's forgiveness,

It can mean that the cross can do something 'for' us, but not do anything 'in' us,

Because forgiveness is more than just a 'get out of hell free' card.

If we think of sin as a legal concept; that we broke some arbitrary rules, for which the punishment we receive is hell when we die; then forgiveness means we are let off our punishment. We are excused of our rightful judgement of hell, and instead invited into heaven when we die.

All a bit 'other worldly'.

All a bit pie in the sky.

Which can lead to a teenage boy wishing he had waited to secure this get out of hell free card until he was closer to dying, because whilst he was happy to be going to heaven, he didn't really want it impacting too much of his life here on earth.

In other words, if sin is a legal concept then forgiveness is a legal concept. It's an idea that isn't rooted in our reality or experience.

But what if we understand that sin is so much bigger than that? What if sin is more than just broken rules? What if we came to see sin as the brokenness we live in, or the destructive cycles that trap us, or the habits that distort us, or the lies we believe, or the stuff we speak out, or the times we resort to power or control? or pride, or self-justification? What if we saw sin as all the times we consume and take rather than give and create? The systems we live in and feed and perpetuate and worship? The stuff we have done and the stuff that's been done to us?

If we see sin as disconnection, dehumanisation, destruction and addiction, then forgiveness is the reversal of these. Forgiveness is reconnection, rehumanisation, restoration and freedom.

Forgiveness isn't just a concept any more.
Forgiveness is a process we are invited in to.
Forgiveness is a process of liberation and reconnection.
Forgiveness is a process of transformation and hope.
Forgiveness is a process of restoration and identity.

Forgiveness is about discovering who we were created to be and breaking free of all the things that trap, distract, and distort us.

Forgiveness isn't just a card we keep tucked away for heaven.
Forgiveness is an invitation to fulfil all our potential here on earth.

If we see sin as disconnection,
dehumanisation,
destruction
and addiction,

then forgiveness is the reversal of these.

Forgiveness is reconnection,
rehumanisation,
restoration
and freedom.

Forgiveness isn't just a concept any more.

Forgiveness is a process we are invited into.

Forgiveness isn't just a concept that kicks when we die, it's a principle of life. It isn't just a one-off event, it's a daily process of freedom and reconnection.

Reconnection with the God who created us. The God who knows us. The God of love, and the God of life.

Reconnection with our true self. The person we were created to be. The fulfilment of all the beauty and creativity that was invested in us.

Reconnection with each other, and the other. Restoring all our relationships, teaching us to see God in each other, learning to prefer, love and value every single person. Learning to agree with God about our enemies when He says that they are beautiful, loved and worth dying for.

Reconnection with creation, learning to value the world around us and find our place in it. Learning to work in harmony with creation rather than against it. Learning to see it as part of us and learning to see ourselves as part of it. Learning to see it as something we are deeply connected with and immersed in, rather than a resource to abuse and control at the expense of others, or at the expense of the planet itself.

This is the forgiveness of the Bible.

One that invites us into relationship with God now. One that restores us and frees us. One that inspires us into forgiveness of others. A forgiveness that inspires us into greater acts of love and hope. Forgiveness that inspires us into more vibrant life, a fuller sense of who we are, a deeper contentment, and an extravagant generosity.

I was at a conference a while ago, and one of the speakers was Brian McLaren, an American writer who, at the time, I knew little about. He was speaking via video conference, so I didn't get to meet him, which was a shame, because there was something he said which sent me spinning. It was something of a throw-away line that hooked me and took me on a journey for the next few months. He said

'Jesus didn't come to set up a forgiveness racket, he came to set up a forgiveness economy'.

There it was. Mid-answer, almost as an aside, but I didn't get any further in his answer. I've no idea what came next, or after that.

So often forgiveness looks like a business. A transaction. If I pray the prayer, give my tithe, obey the rules, attend the church and whatever else is important in that denomination or community, then in return I will receive forgiveness for my sin. It's a package deal. And for all the talk about unconditional love or my salvation being assured, if I were to step out of line, break a rule or even take a different theological line on a hot topic, I could quickly find myself unconditionally out and assured of my place in hell.

But it was exactly this sort of religiosity and legalism which Jesus challenged so strongly. He confronted the religious leaders and condemned them for making God inaccessible. He condemned them for their systems that kept people out, or ashamed or poor, or not good enough. He condemned them for their love of power and control. For their judgmentalism and pride.

Instead Jesus said that as you forgive, so you will be forgiven.

He reminded people to love their neighbour. He challenged those without sin to cast the first stone. He warned people not to judge and He invited us to participate in this Kingdom He announced, not by adhering to the religious systems, but instead by being people of love, forgiveness and prayer. He invited us to join in with the Kingdom by being people of generosity and peace.

He said that our actions matter, not because they meet a legal code, but because they are actions that love, liberate, include, heal, transform and forgive. They are actions that bring life.

Our actions matter because we either perpetuate the systems that oppress and trap and damage people, or we counteract them with practices of love, justice and freedom.

Our actions matter because they either carry on the flow of disconnection and destruction, or they reverse the tide and bring steps of reconnection and restoration.

Our actions matter because they either curse or they bless, and we are created to be a blessing to the whole world.

And so forgiveness, rather than being a concept which kicks in when we die, is a journey we are invited to go on every day, and a beautiful force we are invited to release into the world around us in every situation.

And so, our role

as followers of Christ,

as members of the body of Christ,

is to be reconnected in every way we can,

so that the world around us can be

reconnected,
restored
and renewed

in every way it can.

This is the kingdom of God

confess

Have you ever had one of those situations where something just keeps playing in your mind? A memory? Something that hurt you or offended you? Something someone said to you, or did to you, or didn't do for you when you thought they should have? Or maybe it's something you did once that you feel ashamed of, or you regret. Maybe it's a habit or a behaviour that you can't seem to shake.

And it can be from years ago. Even decades ago.

And it just sits there.

Like a weight.

Like a heaviness you keep dragging around.

And maybe you've become quite good at burying it, or ignoring it, or rationalising it, or pretending it's not really a thing, until someone says something, or you see a comment on Facebook, or a picture on Instagram, or 'that person' does something again, or shows up at the same party, and they're just there laughing like nothing ever happened. Or you're just lying on your bed, or out for a walk and the memory comes out of nowhere. The emotion creeps up on you. The anger or hurt or shame or regret or emptiness or whatever it is, suddenly overwhelms you.

And you don't talk about it.

It's not important. It's water under the bridge. It will go away. It's nothing, it's silly really. It's not worth it.

Or I'm not worth it. I'm nothing. No one really cares.

But it still sits there. Playing like a tape in your head. Over and over. Reminding you of the moment. The emotion. The rejection. The pain.

It grows, and gets deeper into you. And it starts to form you, and deform you. Impacting your words and your thoughts and your actions.

This is what sin does. This is what sin looks like. And the more we hold it in, the more it gets into our soul. It gets into the core of us, and shapes us and corrupts us and distorts us.

In the Psalms David talks about sin and forgiveness.

> 'When I kept it all inside,
> my bones turned to powder,
> my words became daylong groans.
> The pressure never let up;
> all the juices of my life dried up.
> Then I let it all out;
> I said, "I'll make a clean breast of my failures to God."
> Suddenly the pressure was gone—
> my guilt dissolved,
> my sin disappeared.
> These things add up. Every one of us needs to pray.'
>
> The Message

He tells the story of a time when he kept it all hidden away inside, but it felt like death inside him. His bones turned to dust, his words were groans, the life in him ran dry and the pressure built and built.

Sound familiar?

But when he chose to confess, to talk about it, there was instant release. Freedom. His guilt evaporated. He was renewed.

Then he says,

> 'These things add up. Every one of us needs to pray.'

Because these things, however small, build up. They accumulate. And when we've been offended once, it becomes easier to be offended again.

When we have been hurt once, the wound is open, and so other words hurt. Other actions hurt. Maybe things that wouldn't really have hurt in isolation, but now we have a story that says we aren't important, or we aren't good enough, or we are ugly, or bad or unpopular, or unlikeable, or unlovable, or whatever our story says, and it impacts everything we hear. It impacts every situation we are in. And now we hear the same message in every situation.

We see rejection everywhere.

We see failure everywhere.

We see 'not good enough' everywhere.

We see 'not important' everywhere.

We hear condemnation everywhere.

We encounter shame everywhere.

It gets into us.

It gets into our thoughts, and eyes and ears and hearts, and it plays like a tape.

To which David says

'every one of us needs prayer.'

Which is interesting. Because it doesn't say 'every one of us needs to repent'. It says 'every one of us needs prayer.'

It carries a tone of invitation and interaction. It has a feel of hope and relationship and availability. A space where we can be real. A space where we can encounter God. Where we can be healed, loved, restored, changed, liberated, renewed.

In James 5 it says

' Make this your common practice: Confess your sins to each other and pray for each other so that you can live together whole and healed.'

The Message

This moves it from purely an interaction with God, to something we do in community. An invitation into relationship and healing and restoration which happens as we encounter God together.

As we confess to each other, and pray for each other, we are able to be made whole with God, within ourselves, and with each other.

So often when we talk about confession, it can draw up images of children knelt by their beds saying sorry for all the things they can remember doing that day, or monks reciting, or people sat in boxes telling a priest their darkest secrets so that God will forgive them.

But confession is so much more than that, and so much more beautiful and life-giving than we often realise.

If sin is predominantly defined by our legal framework, then forgiveness can be arbitrary and conceptual. If sin is about rules to get into heaven, then forgiveness just kicks in when we die. But if sin is about our brokenness and dehumanisation and disconnection, then, as we have seen, forgiveness is about restoration and reconnection and rehumanisation.

And so confession isn't just talking about the rules we've broken in the hope that God will not hold it against us when we die, but instead confession is about acknowledging all the areas we are disconnected, and broken, and hurting, and lost.
Confession is about recognising where we are less than we were created to be.
Confession is about recognising where shame and hurt and pain and rejection and loss have deformed us and got into our soul.
Confession is about recognising where death has taken root in us and is seeping through us.
Confession is about cutting the tapes that repeat in our heads.
Confession is about confronting our 'not good enoughs' in a belief that we are created to be enough.

Confession is about recognising all these things,

and speaking them out.

Confession is about naming our brokenness,
admitting our pain,
recognising our disconnection,
acknowledging the death inside us,
exposing the walls we have built up,
and then speaking them out of us.

Confession is inviting God in to heal and restore and renew us.

Confession is something we do together, with each other, and with God.

Confession is not a ritual to appease an angry or disapproving God. It is not something that should be driven by a sense of shame and not good enough, but rather by a knowledge that we are loved and accepted and known by the God who created us and knows us completely.

Confession is about being in relationship with people where it is OK to not be OK. It's about being in good relationships, so we can safely talk about, and confess, where we are disconnected and broken and hurting and ashamed. Then we can pray, encounter God together, and be healed, forgiven, restored, reconnected, renewed, and made whole.

judge

I am generally quite a calm parent. Quite laid-back and easygoing. However, once in a while, my children might cross a line, get too loud for too long in an already tense situation, misbehave once too often, or get carried away with excitement at the wrong moment. It is on these rare occasions that I have been known to assume the role of 'Over-Reacting Dad'.

I am certain I am not alone, and at least some of you will have some experience of what I am talking about. Over-Reacting Dad can appear quite unexpectedly in any situation, however it is often when things might seem to be getting out of control. One of my triggers is when Rachel is finding things stressful or difficult, or when she is tired and there is too much noise or chaos.

I respond to these situations like a hero.

Like any hero I am determined to fix the problem as quickly and as efficiently as possible. That requires escalating dramatically and quickly to a loud shout. This is the perfect antidote to noise and chaos and always succeeds in making things worse.

The second aspect of the response is to make irrational threats or directives. These can include anything from 'go to your room and don't make a sound for the rest of the day' to banning meals, to threatening to turn the car round when we have already crossed the Channel, or worse. I am sure you get the idea. Irrational and emotional over-reactions which surprisingly do little to ease Rachel's stress levels.

One such incident happened a few years ago, when our children were little, and they stumbled across our hiding place for Christmas presents. It wasn't a great hiding place, but it had worked well to that point and so there was no real reason to change it. (I should confess at this point that we still use it for some of their presents, but as far as we can tell they must assume that we can't be that stupid and so don't look there).

One of the children found it and then let all the others in on their little discovery. They tried to cover their tracks but Rachel has far too keen an eye for detail and noticed that something had moved. At the inquisition it seemed quite obvious and important to me that I should assume the role of Over-Reacting Dad to emphasise quite how bad and dishonest and wicked my children had been.

The only reasonable course of action I could think of was to ban Christmas all together. All the presents would go back to the shops. No Christmas dinner. No Christmas tree. No Christmas at all.

If anything should teach them not to stumble across presents hid quite obviously, then this was it. For all those 'Modern Family' fans out there, I am aware of the similarity with Phil Dunphy, and I can assure you it's not the only one.

Even as I was saying it, I could feel Rachel giving me a quizzical look of 'what on earth do you think you are saying?'. I remember giving Rachel a sort of 'you're going to have to get us out of this' look back, but I was too far in. I was committed now, and for what it's worth, Over-Reacting Dad seemed to know what he was doing.

The children were obviously distraught, and pleaded with me that Christmas be allowed to continue but Over-Reacting Dad isn't swayed so easily. Even when I would quite like to be. I left the room, confident that my work was done, order was restored and everyone would be better for my effective intervention.

Rachel on the other hand, felt otherwise.

She implemented the standard consequence for bad behaviour, which is time out on the stairs for as many minutes as you are years old. This resulted in an amusing picture of all four kids sat in age order up the stairs, each with their own timer, sitting out the punishment and thinking about what they had done, and how they might change their behaviour in the future. In the meantime, Rachel came to see me, to talk me down from Over-Reacting Dad, back to calm, laid-back, rational Dad, and we decided that maybe banning Christmas wasn't the best or most considered course of action.

Christmas should go ahead after all.

I tell you this story because this is how I think we make God look sometimes. We can present God as Over-Reacting Dad who is angry and wants to punish relatively innocuous looking sins with eternal punishment in the flames of hell.

I remember being told that even if I had just told one lie, it would mean going to hell, which makes 'Over-Reacting Dad' seem like a light-weight.

Sin was sin. Rules were rules. And so God is angry and irrational and Over-Reacting Dad, making threats that He wished He hadn't, but now it was out He had to follow through on it. And so Jesus was our only hope. Loving, rational, and the one who intercedes on our behalf. The one who gets us into heaven. The one who helps us avoid God's punishment. The one who talks God down. The one who talks God round. But only for those who He knows. Everyone else faces the judgement of God.

All of which leaves us feeling like God's punishment is something to be avoided.

God's judgement can often sound like a threat or a warning when we talk about it. One day you will all have to face God's judgement, and if you are found wanting, you will suffer eternal punishment in the flames of hell. Quite a grim and intimidating picture.

Now I should make clear that that I am not dismissing the belief in hell, or separation from God. I am not suggesting that there is no sin, or judgement, or that we shouldn't talk about the consequence of sin. And I'm not saying that there is no consequence to our continued misrepresentation of our creator. That conversation is for another day. I am merely observing how this sort of language and imagery can lead us to an impression that God's judgement is something to be avoided. Something that is faced by the sinners, the rebels and the others, but something that is avoided by the believers in Jesus.

But what if God's judgement isn't like that?

What if, in the same way that this fuller understanding of sin can lead us into new understandings and experiences of forgiveness and confession, it can also reshape how we view judgement?

In the Psalms we see this invitation to God

'Search me, God, and know my heart;
test me and know my anxious thoughts.
See if there is any offensive way in me,
and lead me in the way everlasting.'

NIV

The Psalmist isn't afraid of God's examination or judgement, he desires it. He isn't trying to avoid God's gaze, he is requesting it. He invites God to examine him, to test him, to expose his soul and his innermost being, and then to lead him in paths of healing and restoration. He wants God to examine him, and expose him, so that He can root out wherever there is death in him, and instead choose paths of life and wholeness.

The Psalmist doesn't see judgement as something he has to fear in death, but rather something he desires in life.

What a beautiful idea.

What if we didn't see God's judgement as something to be avoided, but rather something to be sought after or even desired?

What if God's judgement wasn't something to hold back from and hide from, but instead something we could dive into and embrace and submit to?

What if God's judgement wasn't something that destroyed us or condemned us, but instead was something that restored us, and transformed us and liberated us?

What if God's judgement wasn't about death at all?

What if God's judgement was about life in all its fullness?

What if God's judgement was beautiful and life-giving and joyful and extraordinary?

What if God's judgement was the most beautiful journey of hope and transformation?

The Psalmist doesn't see God as angry, or vindictive or violent or against us. Instead he sees Him as loving, gracious, restorative and for us.

The Psalmist shows us a God who 'isn't like that'.

He invites us to know God as a God of justice and wholeness.
A God that can be known.
A God that wants to be with us.
A God whose judgement is good and loving and light.
A God who is in covenant with us.
A God who is committed to us.
A God who is for us and will not leave us.
A God who lays His life down for us.
A God who will never let us go.
A God who is faithful.

Which sounds a lot like marriage.

A covenant between two people which demonstrates commitment, sacrifice, love, and faithfulness. A covenant which invites us to be more. A covenant that invites us to live life fully and generously. A covenant that invites us to take on each other's joy and suffering. A covenant that invites us to be whole.

Which brings us back to the command about adultery.

Adultery matters to God because adultery is about unfaithfulness, when God is faithful and wants us to look like Him.
Adultery matters to God because adultery breaks trust, when God is entirely trustworthy and wants us to look like Him.
Adultery matters to God because adultery breaks us. It causes deep hurt. It damages identity. It shrinks us, and dehumanises us.
Adultery matters to God because marriage is a covenant and covenants matter to God, because how we treat each other, and impact each other and love each other matters.

God is a covenantal God. A God who enters into relationship with us and commits to see it through.

Marriage is a covenant of love, and God is all about love, and God wants us to look like Him.

Marriage is about commitment and connection and deeply giving relationships, which tells us something of what God is like, and God wants us to look like Him.

Marriage is a commitment to pour our whole selves into seeing the other become everything they were created to be. Which is what God does for us.

And so when we break the covenant, we break something profound.
We damage something beautiful.
We diminish ourselves
and our partner
and our family
and our community.

And that matters to God because we matter to God.

Faithfulness matters to God.

God wants to teach us and form paths in us of wholeness and life and beauty together,

because that's what God is like.

eighth

'you shall not steal'

NIV

thief

When I was young, probably around ten years old, I remember having a day off school because I was sick. I don't think I was too sick, but definitely sick enough to convince my Mum that either I was too ill to go to school or I was too ill to be around other children.

I was the youngest and I was quite switched on to the tricks and techniques to swinging a day off, which irritated my brothers no end, but there had to be some benefits to being the youngest. So I had a day off. My Mum had some friends round for coffee in the lounge and I was mainly lying down in my pyjamas in the living room watching TV. I remember going into the kitchen to get a drink, and as I was running the tap to get some water, I could see across the fence into my next door neighbour's garden, where I could see a group of men, all wearing masks and climbing into my neighbour's house through the smashed window. I panicked a little and ducked down so they couldn't see me. Then I scurried out of the kitchen and into the lounge. Now I wasn't supposed to disturb my Mum when she had friends round, and they loved to talk, but I knocked and went in. My Mum glanced at me and carried on talking. I called her, probably slightly frantically but gently. She turned again and told me to wait a minute, and went back to her conversation. I was hopping from one foot to the other like I needed a wee, but I didn't, I just REALLY needed to speak to her.

'Mum!!'

Eventually I managed to distract her long enough to get a mildly frustrated 'What do you want?'

'Mum, there's some burglars next door.'

'Don't be ridiculous darling.'

'I'm not Mum! I saw them. They've smashed the window.'

My Mum gave a little chuckle to her friends to acknowledge how ridiculous I was being, and how funny or cute I was.

'It's probably just workmen darling.'

'Mum they're climbing in the window. They're definitely burglars.'

At this point she decided to come with me to have a look. As we entered the kitchen, I told her to keep down, but she was quite convinced they were workmen and so dismissed my good advice.

'You need to call the police Mum!' I stressed. 'They can catch them.'

But my Mum had other ideas. She walked out into the back garden and up to the fence.

'Cooey!! Excuse me!' she shouted. 'Can I help you? Do you need anything?'

This polite neighbourly intervention was met with language that I wasn't supposed to hear along with shouts of 'Run' and 'Leg it!' and the group of men quickly evacuated the property and ran down the drive and away.

I could not have been angrier. I had told her they were burglars. I had told her what to do. If we had called the police they could have got there quickly and caught them in the act. I could have been a local hero. The burglars could have been caught, and my neighbour's stuff, including my friend's toys and games could have been saved. All would have been well. But instead the police weren't called, the stuff was gone, the burglars were gone and my Mum just looked stupid waving and shouting 'cooey' to a gang of Mancunian criminals.

I decided to take matters into my own hands.

I ran to the front of the house, out the front door, and down the drive to see if I could see where they had gone. I saw them running away down the street and decided to give chase. I was part way down the street in pursuit when I remembered that I was barefoot, and in my pyjamas, which didn't make me feel like I had a good plan if I caught up with them.

I checked back and returned to the house to find my Mum had come up with a fantastic idea of calling the police.

The next couple of hours included police interviews, looking at photos of criminals, driving around the neighbourhood to see if I could recognise anyone from the gang, more coffee with more friends for my Mum, and then a visit from our neighbours.

It turns out that we had disturbed the burglars quite early in their crime and so only a small amount of stuff had been taken, but the emotional damage was obvious.

There was a real feeling of violation. It wasn't just their house or their possessions that had been violated, but my neighbours themselves. They were emotional and shaken and worried. And it didn't go away when they replaced their stuff and fixed their window. It stayed with them for weeks and months.

It wasn't just an attack on their possessions or house, but an attack on their identity, their home, their place of belonging and their security. It was an invasion into their lives.

Because stealing isn't just about possessions, it's about identity and status and security.

In a spiritual and emotional sense, it is a violent and destructive act. It's an act that comes out of greed and discontentment. An act that dehumanises and violates. It is an act that is fed by our sense of not enough. Seeking to gain, not by work or industry or creativity, but by violence and a disregard for the other. For our fellow human. For our neighbour.

In Ephesians it says this

'If you are a thief, quit stealing. Instead, use your hands for good hard work, and then give generously to others in need. '

The Message

Paul takes the law from Exodus which forbids stealing, and then develops it, offering paths of restoration. If you are a thief and you use your hands to steal from people, stop it.

Instead, use your hands for good hard work, and use the proceeds to give generously to others.

Don't use your hands to destroy and take and steal because that diminishes you.

This behaviour is at odds with who you are created to be. It doesn't reflect a God who gives and blesses and pours out. It doesn't reflect a God of generosity and life. A God of creativity and work. And so it shrinks you. It sets you at odds with your creator. It teaches you to use your hands to destroy and take rather than create and give.

And so, instead of this destructive, greed-driven behaviour, God says you should re-purpose your hands into life.

Re-purpose your hands from destroying to creating.

From idleness to work.
From taking to giving.
From stealing to generosity.

Use your hands to work and create and build and contribute to humanity. Contribute to creation. And when you do this, and you receive your rewards for your work, use those rewards to bless others.
Bless the world around you.
Give generously.
Live generously.
Live as people who don't live in lack, but people of gratitude and thankfulness. People who give.

This attitude, this lesson in life, isn't just relevant to us in the obvious acts of theft and burglary,

It teaches us how to approach issues like taxes.
It teaches us how to approach issues like tithing and charity.
It teaches us how to approach environmental issues around resources and green energy.
It teaches us how to approach justice issues around fairtrade, people trafficking, prostitution and pornography.
It teaches us how to be a good boss, or business owner, or employer.

Where are we consuming, or taking, at the expense of someone else?

Where are we benefitting where others are paying the price without their control or consent?

Where are we holding onto our resources when they aren't rightfully ours, or fairly ours?

Where are we not paying our taxes fully, or not giving fully, or withholding our resources from the people we are in community with, in church or in our families?

Where are we using other people for our own ends, or our own pleasure, or our own profit?

Where are we taking more than our fair share, be that at work, in business, at home, in society, or in creation?

Who is suffering because of the life we live, the decisions we make or the way we behave?

Where are we stealing from people, from our community, from our society or from the world?

And how can we change our behaviour and our attitudes so we can repurpose our hands, or our bodies, or our choices to create, and give and be generous, and bless instead of take and destroy and disempower?

Where are we behaving like a thief?

ninth

'you shall not bear false testimony against your neighbour'
NIV

lies

In 2008 Hillary Clinton was making a speech about Iraq at George Washington University. During the beginning of this speech she cited an incident when she was visiting Bosnia in 1996 and said

"I remember landing under sniper fire. There was supposed to be some kind of a greeting ceremony at the airport, but instead we just ran with our heads down to get into the vehicles to get to our base."

The problem is that a number of journalists remembered the trip twelve years earlier, and didn't remember it the same way. They checked back through video footage of the event and found a very different story. The video footage showed a calm landing, with a welcoming party, including a little Bosnian girl reading a poem about how peace had come to Bosnia thanks to Bill Clinton's intervention at an earlier date.

So why would a very smart politician, with great experience, find herself telling a story that is quite easily proven to be mistaken? Why would a street wise politician who is well versed in managing the press, tell a story that is inaccurate when she knows the press in the room would be able to check? Some of them would even remember the trip. It seems like a very careless mistake to make for someone with so much experience.

But what if she thought it was true?

What if she has told that story again and again over time, and it's just been embellished a little each time? What if what actually happened was that there was a comment made to her as she was flying in, that there was some sniper fire in the hills around? What if it wasn't a significant threat to her or the aircraft or the trip, it was just a piece of information she was given? And what if this story evolved a little over time until the sniper fire was aimed at her? What if the welcoming party became a dash into the hangar because it sounded more dramatic? What if it became a convenient truth? And so she allowed it to embellish. Not with the intent of lying, but rather with the desire to emphasise a point or make the story a little more interesting. What if it was just a little harmless exaggeration, but she told the story so many times, that it was no longer embellishment, but now became truth in her own mind? What if it grew into truth in her own memory? What if by the time she told the story in Washington, she wasn't consciously embellishing it, she was just recounting what she remembered?

Would that explain why such an experienced politician recounted a story which was so easily disprovable?

And it's easily done. I've done it myself. Over twenty years ago, I worked at a restaurant in Manchester that was part owned by Mohammed Ali. He came over for the opening night and it was obviously a huge media event. I got to meet him. It was exciting.

Whilst he was walking through the restaurant with people stood around him, his bodyguard did a little spar boxing with him. It was quite a moment for me. Mohammed Ali, who was battling with serious health issues by this point in his life, seemed to spark into life, like instinct kicked in. He threw a couple of punches at his bodyguard. His hands were really fast, and one of them was quite close to where I was stood. It was a really impressive moment to be part of. A real memory. And something great to be able to say you witnessed.

I told this story a few times over the years, as you can imagine, and a couple of years ago I found myself telling the story a little differently. In my version, I said that

'I had shadow-boxed with Mohammed Ali'.

Something jarred within me, because I wasn't sure that this was true, but part of me thought it might be. I realised that I had been telling the story that I had shadow-boxed with Mohammed Ali, for a little while, but when I reflected back on the evening, I realised that I had embellished the story a little. Not massively, but quite significantly. I could see how I had got there. But what I found surprising was that I had to actively revisit the scene to work out what of my memory was true.

My memory had begun to change.

Because when we lie to others, we can wind up distorting our own memories. We can wind up distorting our own perspective of reality.

It is probably one of the less obvious consequences of lying, but it is a significant one. Lying in so many ways seems less 'bad' than some of the other sins, but maybe it's in there for a reason.

Murder and adultery and stealing seem quite obvious rules to be in the list, but lies? Everyone lies sometimes don't they? Doesn't eternal damnation seem a little extreme for such a minor crime? It almost feels like God had nine commands, and He decided that ten is a much better number, and so he added lying, not because it's really bad, but because ten is more memorable.

But I think lying is much more significant than we think.

Not because we have broken a rule, but because of the damage it does.

When I lie to someone a few things happen.

Firstly, and in many ways the most obvious consequence, is that trust is broken between us. If we learn that someone is prone to lying we will be cautious about how much we trust what they say. As a parent, I would often explain to my children that if they did something wrong, such as hit someone, or stole something or broke something, and then lied to me about it, the lie they told was much worse than the thing they had done originally. I would explain that this was because trust between us was a particularly valuable thing. It was so important that we could trust each other. It was important that I knew that when they said something, I could trust that it was the truth, because then we could react in an appropriate way, and should anything else happen in the future, I would know that my child is trustworthy.

Lies break trust between us.

Lies damage our relationships.

Lies build walls between us.

Lies distort our friendships and relationships.

Secondly, lies mislead people.
Lies distort our perception of reality.
They impact how I see the world,
how I see myself,
how I understand things,
and how I perceive other people.

They impact my politics, my friendships, my faith, my approach to work, my enjoyment of life, my understanding of the planet and how things work.

Lies distort people.

Thirdly, as we have seen, they don't just impact our relationship with each other, and how people see the world, they also impact how I see the world, because if I tell a lie often enough, I start to believe it myself.

But why is all this so important?

Why does how I view the world matter?
Surely no-one has a full grasp on reality.
We are all victims of our environment.

Does a lie really matter?

reality

In the gospels Jesus makes a very significant claim.

'I am the Way, the Truth and the Life'
NIV

This is a profound statement and one that we can misunderstand so easily.

It is a statement about how we live, how we see the world and who we are. However, we can so easily make it about what we believe, what we do and what happens when we die.

This statement which is about faith can become about theology. This statement which is about freedom can become about legalism. This statement which is about relationship can become about rules. This statement which is about life, can become about death.

In the same way that we can end up seeking out formula rather than relationship, we can take such a beautiful statement about relationship, rhythm and life and make it about what we believe, what we do, and what happens when we die.

When Jesus declares Himself to be the truth we can often regard it as a theological statement. A comment on the truth of all the things we believe about Him. We think about how He is the Son of God. We think of the truth of His deity, His miracles, His death on the cross, and the truth of His resurrection. We tend to think of it as a statement of belief.

Those things are all true, but I don't think that's what Jesus was talking about.

When we see it that way we can find ourselves developing a static theology. When we see Jesus' statement this way, we can end up fitting it into a belief system that we have to sign up to in order to be acceptable to God, or to get into heaven.

We can make it about a story that happened in the past which we believe in, rather than a past, present and future reality we get to participate in now. And so we can end up making it exclusive or divisive or religious or legalistic, but I don't think that's what Jesus is talking about.

Jesus is talking about something that is all encompassing.

Jesus is talking about something that involves everyone whether they realise it or not. Whether they believe it or not.

Jesus is talking about the reality of everything.

Jesus is talking about how all things are held together in Him.

Jesus is talking about the reality of who God is, who we are, and how the world works.

Jesus is talking about truth in its most profound and complete sense.

It is so much more than theology. It is so much more than just a statement of belief. It is a profound statement of reality. A statement that encompasses all existence. He is stating that the reality of all things is found in Him.

When we align ourselves with Him we align ourselves with reality. When we learn to see the world through His eyes, we increasingly see how things really are.

We see God as He really is.

We see ourselves as we really are.

We see each other as we really are.

We see the other, our enemy, our adversary, as God sees them.

We see creation as it really is.

The brokenness of everything.

We see the deep connectedness of everything.

The truth of everything.

The beauty of everything.

We see the arc towards justice.

We see the arc towards redemption.

We see the arc toward wholeness.

We are invited to join in and nudge those arcs further towards justice and redemption and wholeness.

We are invited to restore and heal and renew and bring life to all creation.

We are invited to be in relationship with the creator of all things.

The truth of all things.

The source of all life.

But the problem is that we aren't aligned with Jesus.

We are all distorted in our view of reality to some degree.

Christians and non-Christians.

We believe lies about ourselves, the world and each other. We buy into ideas that suggest that we aren't enough. We see each other as competition and threat. We find our security, purpose, identity, worth and life from all sorts of things which diminish us. We buy into ideologies and systems of power and control and enmity. We buy into ideas of tribalism and war. We believe in the less we are living in rather than the more we are created for. And so we live at odds with reality.
We live at odds with who we are created to be.

I think this is what Jesus is talking about when he says

"I am the Way, the Truth and the Life'.
NIV

It's not a formula, it's an invitation.

It's an invitation into relationship.

An invitation into life.

An invitation into participation.

An invitation into reality.

aligned

Lies are significant because they distort us and diminish us.

They distort our grasp on reality, which is important because our perspective of reality is what we base our decisions on. As humans we are generally trying to make good decisions. We are trying to make decisions that bring life and fulfilment and make sense of who we are.

Most of the time, most people aren't trying to make bad decisions or destructive choices, but we are skewed in our perspective of reality. We carry around narratives that tell us we aren't good enough. We believe that we are 25% away from having enough.

We try to repair our disconnection by looking to other things to provide us with our sense of purpose or identity or security or life or hope or whatever it is we feel is missing. We believe the systems that trap us in cycles of poverty, or power or control. We buy in to the mindsets that tell us that we should be suspicious of others, or that we should overpower or dominate or compete. We give space to our addictions and our fears. We distract ourselves and diminish ourselves, and so when we are presented with lies and misdirections, they add to our distortions. They add to our fears and our doubts. They add to our narratives. And so instead of choosing love, or life, or truth, or wholeness, we find ourselves making choices that damage us.

If I believe that I am not good enough, or ugly, or unlovable or bad, then I will live out that story. When I am presented with an opportunity for affection or attention, I will dive in. I will take what I can, even if it's destructive in the long term, because my need to be loved or needed or desirable is so strong in me.

If my biggest fear is being seen as weak or insignificant, then when I am presented with an opportunity to impose myself, or prove my worth or my strength or my significance, then I may well take it with both hands, with little concern for who might get hurt or damaged in the process.

If I am overwhelmed by my fears, or mistakes, or stories of failure or abuse, or rejection, then I might turn to anything that will distract me from the deep pain that is inside me. However addictive or destructive it might be.

The story we believe we live in defines our behaviour.

And lies distort our story.

But if we can find paths of restoration, however long or painful, then there is hope.

If we can dare to believe that Jesus invites us into that relationship as we are, with all our baggage and brokenness and fear and pain and addiction and emptiness and worthlessness, then we can take steps towards a better reality.

If we can find the courage to dive into the relationship Jesus invites us into, then over time we can be healed and restored. Over time we lose some of our distortions and distractions, and gradually align ourselves with Jesus. We align ourselves with truth and reality.
We can enter into the beautiful and complete acceptance of God.
We can learn to see things as Jesus does.
We can learn to see what God is really like,
A God of love and beauty and grace and hope.
A God who is with us and for us.
A God who heals and restores us.

And as He does, we learn to see ourselves as God sees us.
We learn to see ourselves as God created us to be.

Loved.
Accepted.
Included.
Beautiful.
Of immense worth.

Someone who carries God's DNA.

Someone who is created to create and bless and love and heal and restore and give and speak life into the world around us.

And as we grow in this reality, we learn to see the other as God sees them.

Loved.

Accepted.

Included.

Beautiful.

Of immense worth.

Someone who carries God's DNA.

Someone who is created to bless and love and heal and restore and give and speak life into the world around them.

A partner in Christ.

A brother.

A sister.

Family.

As we enter into relationship with Jesus, allowing ourselves to be changed by Him, engage with Him, converse with Him, and spend time with Him, then we will gradually align ourselves with Him.

We will become like Him.

As we allow the Spirit of God to work in us and through us, we will demonstrate more love, life, hope, beauty, patience, kindness and goodness.

We will become more like Him.

We will learn to see the world as He sees it.

We will see new colours.

We will hear new melodies.

We will encounter new experiences of life and joy.

Aligning ourselves with God is a journey that takes a lifetime.

And it's new every day.

We aren't aligning ourselves with something static, like a theology.

We are aligning ourselves with someone dynamic.

Someone who is new every morning.

Someone who changes every day.

Now, I know that is a little controversial, because I am sure you are pointing out that God never changes, and so let me explain a little.

I believe in a God who is unchanging, eternal, consistent and complete. But I also encounter a God who is new every morning.

A God who never stops changing.

He changes because I change.

And so, because we are in relationship, He accommodates and adjusts and changes with me. He changes because the world around me changes and so He shifts and flexes and shows me new things, and new experiences, and new perspectives every day.

The unchangeable God who is perpetually changing.

Because that's what relationship does. It changes us. It draws us in and moulds us. And so I believe that God changes. Not because He has to, or because He is incomplete in some way, but because He chooses to, because He desires and loves relationship, and He gives Himself into it.

He gives Himself to me.

He commits.

Covenant.

Love.

Selflessness.

Beauty.

Life.

Sacrifice.

Hope.

Vulnerability.

A God who is vulnerable.......

Now that's a God worth knowing.

tenth

'You shall not covet your neighbour's house. You shall not covet your neighbour's wife, or his male or female servant, his ox or donkey, or anything that belongs to your neighbour.'

NIV

contentment

In a world where we are taught to compare and compete with everybody else, the idea of contentment is a radical one.
In a world where we are taught to win, and accumulate, and have the most, and consume, the idea of contentment is a radical one.
In a world where we are all 25% away from having enough, the idea of contentment is a radical one.
When a nation of slaves have only ever known oppression and lack and poverty and slave labour, the idea of contentment is a radical one.

But this is what the Israelites were presented with.

And it's an interesting command to finish on.

The previous commands have been about actions.
Don't steal. Don't kill. Don't commit adultery. Don't lie.

All actions.

But this command isn't about an action, it's about the heart.
It's about an attitude.
It's about how we see the world.
It's about how we see ourselves.
It's about identity
It's about how we see the reality of everything.

This group of commands which seem to be about what we do, ends on a command about who we are.

From actions to identity.
From behaviour to heart.
From doing to being.

Which all points to Jesus.

Jesus takes up the baton on this when He delivers His Sermon on the Mount. He reflects back on the command not to kill, and says that in the kingdom He is declaring, we should not hate. Because hate is an attitude. It's a heart issue. And it's a heart issue that prompts and causes the action to kill. Our desire to kill stems from our hearts. Our actions reflect what's in our heart. They reflect our story. They reflect how we see the world.

Jesus says it's not enough to just follow the rule of not killing people, what God is interested in is our hearts. Do we hate people? Because when we hate, we dehumanise. When we hate, we put ourselves in a position where we are at odds with God.

We disagree with God.

God, who IS love, loves us. And He loves our enemies.

Which is why He tells us to love our enemies. Because we are created to look like Him. God sees our enemies and our opponents as beautiful. He thinks they are worth dying for. He thinks they are stunning.

And so when we set ourselves against them, we set ourselves against God.

When we declare them worthless or irrelevant or nothing, then we dehumanise them. We speak death over them. We curse them. And God calls us to be people who speak blessing and life.
God calls us to love like He does.
God calls us to forgive.

Continually and repeatedly.

Forgive.

Jesus talks about the command that says 'you shall not commit adultery'. Jesus says that instead, in the new kingdom He is announcing, we shouldn't lust. Adultery is an action, but lust is a heart issue.
Lust is an identity issue.
Lust comes from a sense of dissatisfaction.
Lust comes out of not enough.

As we saw in Love Actually, the command is insufficient. The law is not enough in itself. We can end up just following the letter of the law and missing the point of it. Our actions come from our hearts. The problem is in our hearts.

Love is about giving ourself to the other. Love is about pouring ourselves into seeing our wife or husband become everything they were created to be. Love is about us pouring ourselves out for the people around us to see them fulfil their potential and their beauty.

Love is always about giving.
Love is always generous.
Love is always outward.
Love leads us towards feeling complete and whole and more.

Lust, on the other hand, takes.
Lust desires for my own satisfaction.
Lust consumes and distorts and abuses and diminishes.
Lust shrinks us.
Lust sees the other as a resource to be used.
Lust is harsh.
Lust is selfish and self-serving.
Lust can be violent and aggressive.
Lust leaves us feeling dissatisfied and less.

When we are created to give, to bless, and to reveal God to the world around us, lust teaches us to consume and dehumanise and hurt.

And so Jesus says that this is a heart issue.

And He goes further.

When He is asked about which command is the greatest, He answers with two commands.

Love God.

Love others.

He then says,
ALL the law hangs on these two scriptures.
ALL the law is about love.
ALL the law is a heart issue.
ALL the law is about identity.
ALL the law is about who you are, rather than what you do.
ALL the law is about who we are, and who we are created to be.

God isn't a God who is wanting to condemn us, or make us fail, or trip us up, or catch us out. God is a God who is always inviting us into relationship, and into a fuller reality of who we truly are.

Sin is all the ways in which we fall short of our humanity. Sin is all the ways in which we make ourselves less human. Less than we were created to be. And so God continually invites us into greater humanness. Greater identity. Greater reality.

This is why contentment is so important.
This is why contentment is so radical.

The opening command talks about the identity of God. God as the source of life, and beauty, and creativity, and love. God as the source of security, and purpose, and identity, and status. The second and third commands then talk about us as conduits of this blessing and life. Conduits of beauty, and hope, and love. Co-creators with God. Invited into participation. Image bearers of God. Visible representations of the invisible God.

The more we align ourselves with our creator, align ourselves with God, the more we will be people who reflect God's beauty.
People who reveal what God is really like.
People who bring life into a room or a community.
People who bring hope into the darkest situations.
People who forgive.
People who include.
People who are generous.
People who are kind.
People who persevere and people who don't give up.
People who see the beauty and the spark in people, however deeply buried it might be.
People who know who they are.
People who are content.

comparison

Have you ever had to work with someone that you just didn't get on with? Or be in a sports team with someone you couldn't stand? Or maybe there's someone in your church who just irritates you. And sometimes the other people don't see it. But this character dominates everything. Whatever is going on, whatever you're doing, there they are.

In my youth group, there was a guy like this. He was called Andrew. We got on for most of the time, but there was one year where we did not. It started because we liked the same girl. She was called Holly. Holly was beautiful and cool and funny. Everyone felt better when they were around her. I was crazy about her, and so was Andrew. I didn't hide my admiration or affection for her, but neither did Andrew. And to be fair, he demonstrated more commitment to the cause than I did, but to me it felt a bit weird. He would call her all the time. He would send her letters. He would ride to her house and take a picnic so he could spend the day nearby, all on the off-chance of seeing her. He was definitely committed.

One area where I did have an advantage was football. Andrew was gangly and awkward and didn't have great coordination, but he tried hard. I, on the other hand, was pretty good. I remember one day when we were having a kick-about after church. It mattered because the girls were watching, including Holly. Andrew was on the other team. Things weren't going great, and I think we were losing. I picked the ball up in midfield and started on a run. I was quite a mazy dribbler and rated my chances at running through the whole team to score a wonder goal. In front of Holly too, who would naturally realise how irresistible I was. I was progressing well with my mazy run when Andrew decided to get involved.

He was all over my back, grabbing me and pulling me, and at one point, actually on my back, causing me to effectively give him a piggy-back. I tried to shake him off, and in doing so, my elbow caught him flush in the eye. I really wasn't trying to elbow him. I was just trying to throw him off, but there was probably more frustration than just the fact that he was clumsily trying to tackle me. The shrugging off probably also contained a significant amount of anger and irritation from the previous days, weeks and months.

Andrew fell to the floor screaming and clutching his eye which was already swelling nicely. Girls came running on to the field to see if he was OK. Holly rushed to his side, giving me a scolding glare that said 'How could you?'

And then Andrew took a break from his wailing to say that he was sure I hadn't done it on purpose. He had no hard feelings.

Perfect.

Now he wasn't only the victim, but he was the good guy too. And I was the bad guy. All the girls, including Holly, gave him even more attention now. Telling him how nice he was and running to get ice packs and giving him cuddles. I had to walk off, game abandoned, having lost in every way possible.

They get into your head don't they? You find yourself thinking about them a disproportionate amount of time. You can't stand it when they get praise, or recognition, or profile, or success. You can't bear it when they score a goal, or make a great tackle, or the boss singles them out for praise. You can't bear it when they get a spot in the worship team or on the teaching rota. They ruin everything for you. They tarnish everything. Even the great moments are spoiled because they're there.

They have a disproportionate amount of influence over you and your emotional wellbeing.

If you recognise this, you should probably go back and read the chapter on forgiveness, but don't despair too much, because the disciples had this problem too.

In the book of John we get an insight into some of the tensions in the group of disciples. John, as the writer of the book, doesn't refer to himself as John. Instead, he refers to himself as

'the disciple whom Jesus loved'.

It wasn't unusual for writers at this time to create a reference for themselves, but it is interesting that John chose to refer to himself in this way.

It just sounds quite arrogant.

Did it mean that Jesus didn't love the others?

Did it mean that he was Jesus' favourite?

This might explain why John's was the last gospel written and our earliest copies were written after all the other disciples had died.

You wonder how they might have reacted.

It certainly seems that Peter may have felt that John got an easy ride from Jesus. It does seem that there was some rivalry between them. One example of this comes towards the end of the gospel. After Jesus' resurrection, He meets His disciples on the shore as they get back from a fishing trip. He makes a point of speaking to Peter, because Peter is the one who betrayed Jesus three times. And so three times Jesus asks Peter if he loves Him.

Three times Peter says he does.

Three times Jesus commissions him to be an apostle in the new kingdom. To lead and teach and serve the followers of Jesus. This is a beautiful moment of restoration. Jesus doesn't condemn Peter for his betrayal, He redeems him. He restores him. It's a really stunning moment. Jesus then prophesies over Peter, about his life and death.

Can you imagine that?

Having a one-on-one with Jesus and Jesus forgives you, restores you and commissions you, and then prophesies over you.

What a moment.

But Peter isn't happy with the prophesy that Jesus has for him. It sounds like a difficult end to his life. It sounds like suffering. So Peter, instead of focusing on Jesus, looks around and sees John.

The guy who's always there. The guy who can't do anything wrong. The annoying kid. Teacher's pet. His nemesis.

Peter turns and sees John, and points at him and asks Jesus,

'What about him?'

Comparison kills us.

We spend our lives comparing ourselves to each other.
We spend our lives asking 'What about him?'
We spend our lives chasing the bigger yacht. The 25% more.
We spend our lives competing with each other and comparing ourselves to each other.

As a youth leader it became evident that in any group of girls, each girl would think that the other girls were all beautiful, but they themselves were ugly. It happens time and time again. Am I as beautiful, or as clever, or as rich, or as successful as my neighbour or my competitor? Am I driving a better car, or living in a better area, or in a better career, or eating in better restaurants, or shopping in better shops?

And then there's our kids.

Are my kids more beautiful, or smarter, or walking sooner, or talking sooner, or achieving more, or more popular, or going to a better school or university, or in a better career, or living in a better area?

Because if we carry any disappointment with our own lives, then we might project our dreams onto our children.

Or, if we view ourselves as successful in our own lives, then we might demand a certain level of achievement, or success from our children, to reinforce our own perceived success.

And we pass it on, and we pass it on. All the way down through the generations. Discontentment. Not enough. Pressure. Expectation.

And expectation kills joy. Every time.

And it kills us.

In the tenth commandment we are given a list of things we are not allowed to covet. Now, I don't know about you, but I haven't found myself coveting my neighbours donkey recently. Or my neighbours ox. Or their servants. It seems like quite an outdated list. But if we dig into it, we might get an idea of what that might look like today.

A man's wife was to do with his family, and his heritage. She was to do with status and security. She was to do with life and belonging. She was to do with name and identity. And so, we might look in the same way today at our families. Our partners and our children. Our hopes and our dreams. Our ambitions all being tied up with the security of our families. And so, to covet or take someone's wife, or husband, or partner, is to break up that security and identity. To compare your family, or partner, or situation to theirs, is a destructive thought process.

It breaks up your own security and identity. To wish you were married to somebody else, or that your husband did the things your friend's husband does, can eat into you and destroy your marriage too. To envy people you love can build walls between you. It can destroy relationships. And it shrinks you.

Male and female servants were a sign of wealth and standing in society. They said something of your status or your position. And so, today it might be to do with titles, or roles in society. It might be to do with wealth, or character, or reputation. Things we might covet or desire in others. And when we do this, it diminishes us and shrinks us again. We devalue who we are, and our own character or reputation. We breed dissatisfaction within ourselves, and we can often find ourselves looking for ways to damage the other person's standing, or reputation, or status. Which means we stop being someone who blesses, and encourages, and commits to seeing the other become everything they can be. Instead we want to pull down, and criticise, and diminish them.
We can destroy their identity, rather than forming our own.
We pursue their identity, rather than pursuing our own.

People had an ox as a means of income. It would help them work the ground, produce a crop and earn a living. So, we might look at that as a career or a salary. Which is something we can often find ourselves comparing, or envying, or coveting. We compete in business all the time. We look at the people ahead of us and imagine that we could do a better job, or be more successful. We compare our salaries, or the symbols that suggest our wealth. We talk about their weaknesses and vulnerabilities. Or maybe, we just admire someone else and what they do. We wish we could do something similar, but we don't believe we can, and so we just sit in our own dissatisfaction and our feeling of not enough.

A donkey was a means of transport. People would have a donkey to travel long distances. It is how they would get about. So, instead of a donkey, we might think of a car or a holiday. For me it would be an Audi R8. I would just love to drive one for the joy of it. For the experience. I just think they're so beautiful. They're so well designed. They ooze beauty and quality and power. I will confess to times when I may have coveted an Audi R8, but it makes more sense than coveting my neighbour's donkey.

And then, as the Bible does so often, it puts in a catch at the end.

'Anything else that belongs to your neighbour.'

What are the things that we find ourselves coveting, or desiring, or thinking about a little too often?
What are the things about our friends, or our colleagues, or our neighbours, or the celebrities we follow, that make us feel worse about ourselves?
What are the things that breed discontentment in us?
What are the things that cause us to feel not enough?
Who are the people we look at and wish we were them?

Or, do we resent them because they had more opportunity than us, or better parents than us, or were born smarter, or prettier than us? Do we resign ourselves to less, whilst convincing ourselves that if we had their opportunities, or upbringing, or friends, or looks, or brains, or whatever it is, then we would be happy too? Because you know that's probably not true right? We have already seen that the more we have, the less content we seem to be. When we get the 25%, we still feel 25% away.

So why do we look at other people's lives and wish we were them? What is it that drives this competition in us that keeps telling us to push harder, and succeed more, and be more?
Why do we find ourselves wishing we were as rich as them? Or as successful as them, or as beautiful as them, or as happy as them? What is it that means we look at our neighbour, or colleague, or the guy next to us in church, or the girl on the TV, or the family on the street, and find ourselves wishing we were them, or like them? Or, do we thank our lucky stars that we aren't them? Do we convince ourselves that we are better than them because of our perceived success, or beauty, or wealth, or whatever it is that we measure stuff by?

Because sometimes we compare to make ourselves feel better. And sometimes, we don't stop at comparing, we take steps to steal, or to take their job, or their wife, or their possessions, or their success.

And we become a thief.

Sometimes, we criticise them and find fault with them just to make ourselves feel better.

But none of this is good.
It all comes out of comparison.
It all comes out of feeling not good enough.
It all comes out of not knowing who we are.

Rachel, has a favourite quote she uses, by Bill Johnson,

> 'If you knew who God made you to be,
> you'd never want to be anyone else'.

And I'm not talking about being perfect, or not having any issues. Because we all have issues. We are all still working through stuff. But to know who we are; to be working towards who we were created to be; to know God in relationship, and to find our identity, and purpose, and security, and status, and life in Him.....

That's a beautiful thing.

Can you imagine that?

Finding contentment to that extent? Being so assured of who you were created to be that you didn't see anyone else as a threat, or competition, or a rival?

Can you imagine if you didn't spend your time resenting people, or wishing you were them? Can you imagine how it would feel if you didn't need to rationalise someone else's happiness, because if you had their money, or their family, or their career, or their house, or their children, or their parents, or their background, or whatever it is, then you would be happy too?

Can you imagine how liberating that would be?

It's not about what we have, or what we do. The things we have or don't have aren't the secret to contentment.

Contentment isn't about possessions or wealth,
it's about who we are.
It's about identity.

Wherever you go, and whatever you do, there you are.
The one thing you can't escape, is you.
We tend to follow ourselves around.

I see so many people who are unhappy, and so they try to change their circumstance before they try to change themselves.

They get a new hairstyle, or new clothes or a new car. They apply for a new job, or they move house, or they move towns or they move church, or they get new friends.

But wherever they go, there they are.

Whatever problems we have, tend to go with us. And so sooner or later they show up again, and again, until we find the courage to deal with them.
Until we choose to change.
Choose to forgive.
Choose to be healed.
Choose to be restored.
Choose to let go of the thing that was said about us or done to us.
Choose paths of confession and repentance.
Choose paths of forgiveness and wholeness.
Choose paths of identity.
Choose paths of relationship with our creator.

Because then we will learn contentment.

Because then we will know who we are.

humility

Humility is an interesting word. I hear it used a lot, but I think we can often misunderstand it.

In the book of Numbers, Moses is described as being the most humble man that ever lived, which is a nice thing to say about someone, until you realise that the book of Numbers is often credited to Moses. If that were the case, it would mean that Moses described himself as the most humble man that ever lived. Which sounds like a bit of an oxymoron. How can the most humble man to ever live, boast about being the most humble man? Surely that would disprove his point almost instantly.

I remember spending a week at a Bible college when I was about ten years old. My Dad was teaching for a week and I went along. It was a lot of fun. I got to hang out with all the students, who came from all over the world. I got to spend meal times with them and free time. We played football, croquet, giant chess, card games, and mini golf.

Probably my clearest memory was the golf. I was watching some American students play. There was lots of laughter, and they were quite competitive, but there is a phrase they kept using which stuck in my head. It would be used every time they missed a shot, and it would be particularly passionately exclaimed if they only just missed. If the ball rolled around the lip of the hole and stayed out. Every time they missed, or lost a hole, they would say,

'The Lord has humbled me'.

I'm not aware I had ever heard this phrase before, and I knew they were using it in a light-hearted way, but it stuck with me. It played in my head. What did they mean? Was God making them miss shots? Were they blaming God for their poor aim? Or were they suggesting that God wasn't just making them miss, but was intentionally making them miss to humble them? And if so, why? And in what way does it humble them?

Were they suggesting that God was making them miss golf shots on a mini golf course to remind them of how useless they were without Him?

Was God really that insecure?

Does God really care about a meaningless game of golf?

Is God really going to intervene in the path of a golf ball to teach some American students a lesson about humility?

And if God is controlling all the balls and all the shots then what's the point in playing?

It doesn't say anything about you at all. It just says something about who God is, or who He likes most, or how controlling He is.

Is humility really about realising that you're not very good at stuff?

Is humility really about talking yourself down?

In the nine months running up to taking on the leadership of the church, I spent some time in Brazil. I had been to Brazil a couple of times before, but on this trip I was going out to take part in a conference about church for the marginalised. A conference about how the various tribes and groups and outcasts and minorities can work together, and bless each other, and include each other. A conversation about how we can see Jesus in and through each other. They are fabulous events that often leave me wondering how I get to be part of it. Thousands of people from all different walks of life.

Hell's Angels, hippies, circus performers, goths, musicians, people who work in the sex industry, people who intervene in people trafficking, people from the favelas of Brazil, pastors who lead churches in prisons and drug dealer's houses, people from the mountains of Peru, from the tribes of the Amazon, hip-hop artists, graffiti artists, underground movements,

and then me. A 'nearly' church leader from Somerset.

I didn't know it was possible to feel so out of your comfort zone, and so privileged at the same time.

It is an extraordinary experience to be bear-hugged by a seven foot, three hundred pound hell's angel who is crying because he's so pleased to see you.

It is quite an amazing privilege to sit and listen to a guy who has been rescued from prostitution and addiction, and now risks death most nights as he tries to rescue others.

And nothing can prepare you for being driven through the favelas of Rio at night, with an ex-international drug dealer, not stopping at red lights because apparently driving through the red lights is safer.

'If we drive through the red lights, maybe we die,' he said.
'If we stop, we die.'

When his drug-laden ocean liner heading to Europe was intercepted by Interpol, he fled to the Amazon where he met an eighty year old missionary lady who told him about Jesus, and he decided to give his life to Christ. As did his porn star wife, and his kids. Now, having sold all his homes around the world, all his possessions and given the money away, he spends his days serving as a hard-up pastor to drug addicts in the most dangerous streets in Brazil.

Apparently, it's the least he could do.

Anyway, back to the story. For two or three years I had been praying for humility and wisdom. This might sound like a strange thing to do, but someone had given me a picture or a word saying that God wanted me to have humility and wisdom so I could be prepared for whatever it was He was calling me to do, and so I should always pray for it. And so I did. It felt like a fairly reasonable and risk-free thing to do. So every time anyone asked if they could pray for me about anything, I would always ask that they pray for humility and wisdom. This went on, as I say, for two or three years, until the day before I flew to Brazil. A lady in my church asked me, on the Sunday morning, if there was anything she could pray for me for my trip. I obviously replied, asking her to pray for wisdom and humility, as I always did. She said 'OK', and we closed our eyes and I waited for her to start praying.

But she didn't.

There was a long silence. Until I opened my eyes, when I saw her looking at me with a slightly confused look on her face.

I asked if there was a problem and she replied,

'God says I can't pray for humility and wisdom for you. You already have it. You're wearing it. It's all over you. Is there anything else I can pray for?'

I was a bit confused. I didn't feel particularly wise or humble. As you can imagine, the thought of taking on the role of leading the church had me feeling like I needed all the help I could get.

It wasn't that I thought I should feel humble in an 'I'm nothing, or nobody, or not good enough' sort of way. I just didn't know how I should feel.

I felt like this was what I was created to do and called to do, I just didn't know if I wanted to do it.

I wasn't self deprecating. I just had the sense that this was all God's idea, He must know what He's doing, so all I had to do was let Him do it.

So, when she said she couldn't pray for those things, I was quite confused, because I didn't feel any different. I didn't feel like I had all the answers. But I didn't feel like I wasn't good enough either.

When I was in Brazil, at the conference, I remember a particular speaker. He was a crazy guy, from Holland I think, and he was a high octane speaker. He told a story about humility, and how God kept teaching him to rely on Him. He told crazy stories of impossible situations where God had done the miraculous. I don't remember the stories particularly except one involved a bridge, but I do remember it was about humility. At the end he asked for a response. Anyone who wanted more humility should come forward for prayer.

I didn't wait around. This was my bag. Humility is exactly what I was supposed to pray for and ask for.

I went forward, as did about two hundred others. He asked us to kneel as he prayed for us.

So I knelt.

And then, as he started praying, I felt God ask me 'What are you doing?'

I tried to shush Him a bit, because I was praying, and I told Him that I was praying for humility, as He had told me to do.

'Get up!'

'What?' I replied.

'Get up!' I've told you that you have humility, now get up and go back to your seat.'

'You're kidding me right?'

'Get up now, and go back to your seat.'

So I had to stand up, and tip-toe my way through the hundreds of people around me and walk back to my seat to sit back down. I am sure that they were all a little confused as to why I had suddenly decided I didn't need humility any more. So was I.

How can praying for humility be wrong?

During the break I went to seek out the speaker, partly because I felt like I probably needed to explain myself, but also because I wanted answers. I told him the story and then asked him 'In what way do I have humility? Because I don't feel humble at all.'

His answer was profound.

'Humility isn't a feeling. Humility is the recognition that it's all God.'

Humility is linked to obedience. We do the things God calls us to do, in whatever situation we are in, however crazy, however ridiculous, and we recognise that God does it all. It's only dependent on my obedience, not my ability. It's all God. He does it all. We just get to go along for the ride.

That was the moment that I realised that God had been teaching me humility all along. Not the self-deprecating, helpless, 'not enough' form of false humility, but a deep knowledge of who I am in Him. A deep understanding of my identity, as a consequence of a deep understanding of who God is.

Humility is all about identity. Coming to terms with our true self, and learning to let go of our false self. Coming to terms with who I am created to be, and learning to let go of all the lies I have absorbed, or inherited, or adopted from the world around me. Which makes more sense of the idea that Moses, if he had written Numbers, could have declared himself to be the most humble person to live. Moses just knew who he was and who he wasn't any more.

When we think we are being humble, when we self-deprecate and talk ourselves down, we miss the point significantly. This is just another form of pride. False humility.

Often, we are seeking affirmation or praise from people. Sometimes, we are just projecting onto ourselves what we fear other people are thinking, with the idea that if we say it first, we can disempower it. But instead we reinforce it, and we let the lie take root in us. Our suspicions become our self-imposed realities.

God isn't the God who humbles us by deviating our golf balls, or making us fail, or making us feel worthless, or not good enough. God is the God who humbles us by teaching us who we are.

Humility is about identity.

He humbles us by showing us who He is, and who He has created us to be.
He humbles us by showing us the reality of everything. The beauty, and the potential, and the gifting, and the life, and the creativity He has created us for. And then by teaching us to find our source of this in Him.
Teaching us to know who we are in Him.
It's all from Him.
It's all Him.

He just invites us along for the ride.

calling

I have something of a phobia of food.

Not all food. I love meat. I love sugar, which is a problem as I am diabetic. But I do not like vegetables. In fact I hate most vegetables. Not in a 'I'd rather not eat them' sort of way. More in a 'I will vomit and cry' sort of way. Which is what would tend to happen as a child, and I will still have a not dissimilar reaction. And it's not just vegetables. I tend to like quite plain food, and I really don't like spicy food, or unusual food. I can't really deal with Mexican food or Indian food. I love Brazilian BBQ, but other Brazilian food does not work.

I really must deal with that one day.

The reason I tell you, is because it's a real issue for me. It impacts all sorts of things. It makes me fearful or going to other people's homes for dinner. It means I have control issues around food. It influences my health. It influences how we eat together as a family. It influences a lot of things.

As a child, it influenced my prayers quite a bit. Not because I was asking God to make me like vegetables, which would have been quite a smart thing to do, but instead because I was afraid that God might call me to be a missionary in a far away country. And if He did that, how would I survive with the food? So, I became quite concerned that God would make me do something that I hated, or just couldn't do. Which makes God sound quite mean or vindictive. But this was my fear as a child.

By the time I went to Bible college, the idea of God asking me to be a missionary had become far less scary than being asked to lead a church. This again came out of fear, but this time the fear came out of pain. I had been hurt by the church. I had been rejected by the church. The church was a scene of failure, and rejection, and hurt, and brokenness for me. And so I just didn't want to go back there.

I would do anything for God, even be a missionary and learn to get over my phobia of food. But the one thing I asked was, don't make me lead a church.

I think we can see calling like this sometimes. When we think about what God is calling us to, we imagine He is going to call us to do something crazy or outrageous, or completely out of our comfort zone. All of which may be true. But do we tend to look at other people, or hear their story, and be horrified, because what if God called me to do that? It would be my worst nightmare. It's just not what I would ever want to do. It makes no sense of me.

Exodus tells the story of Moses. As we have seen, Moses is the guy who God calls to free the Israelites from their slavery in Egypt and lead them through the wilderness to the promised land. To bring freedom to the oppressed. To bring peace and identity to a nation. To lead them on a journey of liberation.

The beginning of this story shows Moses being taken into the Egyptian royal household as a baby. A position of privilege and influence while the rest of his people were slaves. You can imagine he grew up with a few identity issues. A child in the royal household. Brothers with the Pharaoh in waiting. And brothers with the slaves that were building the storehouses. It's easy to imagine that he might feel that it would fall on him to save his people. He might well believe that it was his calling to change the future of his people. To bring peace. To restore their identity.

One day Moses talks a walk to see his people working. You can sense the identity crisis in him. You can feel the longing that he feels. To do something. To be with his people fully. To save them. Whilst he is watching them work, he sees an Egyptian beating a Hebrew slave and he reacts.

He intervenes and kills the Egyptian.

I imagine there was a lot of pent up emotion and pain in that moment. I imagine it wasn't just about the incident itself, but more about his continued angst, and disconnection as a Hebrew, growing up in the palace, like a child of Pharaoh, as a brother of the Pharaoh in waiting, whilst his true brothers suffered and died. The pain of having everything while his family had nothing.

The trauma of being in the place of power, and yet being totally powerless to change the fate of the people he cared about most.

The agony of sensing his calling, and being unable to do anything about it.

And so he snaps.

He reacts. He intervenes to liberate his Hebrew brother, and he kills the Egyptian. He panics, and he hides the body in the sand. He buries his guilt, and he carries on like nothing has happened. But everything has changed.

The next day he goes back, to see his people again. Maybe he just wanted to feel connected to them. Maybe he wanted to pretend like nothing had happened. Maybe he thought that news might have spread, and he might be viewed as some sort of hero. Some sort of saviour. Or maybe he just wanted to be where he felt most at home in a moment of intense pain and stress.

But he went back.

Because sometimes that's what we do when there's something we're ashamed of. Sometimes that's what we do when we have a deep pain. We keep going back to it. Revisiting it. Playing it over in our minds. Picking at the scab. Not confessing it, or constructively trying to move on or heal, just sitting in it. Punishing ourselves or beating ourselves up. Consumed with guilt, and regret, and shame, and failure. It eats away at us. It shrinks us. It diminishes us. It consumes us.

This time, Moses is confronted with two Hebrew slaves arguing with each other. Again he intervenes, this time to try and bring peace.

But it goes wrong again.

Rather than being grateful, or responding well, they confront Moses, asking him if he is going to kill them like he killed the Egyptian. They have completely misunderstood his heart.
They have misunderstood his motivation.
They have misunderstood his calling.

He wants to save them, not kill them.
He wants to bring peace, not division.
He is for them, not against them.

Again, he panics, and this time he runs. If they know, then more people know. And soon Pharaoh will know, and that won't go well. His conflict and his pain will be exposed. His guilt and shame will be known. His crisis of identity will be his downfall.
Pharaoh will kill him.

Rejected by his Hebrew brothers. Hunted by his Egyptian brother.

He runs.

He flees the country, alone, lost, abandoned and failed.
Failed as an Egyptian and failed as a Hebrew.
Failed as a saviour and failed as a peacemaker.
Failed.
He messed everything up. Got everything wrong.

Have you ever felt like that?
Like, whenever you try to do something right it goes badly wrong. Like, whenever you try to step up and step into who you think you're supposed to be, you just get shot down. Your greatest dream becomes your greatest nightmare. Your greatest ambition becomes your greatest failure. The scene of your destiny becomes the scene of your pain and shame.

This is Moses' story. And so he runs and doesn't go back. He starts life again in Midian. He works, tending sheep in the wilderness for a man who becomes his father-in-law. And he settles. He makes a life. Things are OK. He's happy. Egypt is in the past, never to be revisited. He has a family and a job and a life in Midian. And it's OK. It's not everything he was called to, or created for, but it doesn't hurt the same. It doesn't feel as painful. All Egypt holds for him is regret and disappointment. At least in the wilderness, he has a family and a life.

But the writer tells us he goes to Midian, and Midian means 'strife', or 'contentious' or 'contended', which maybe points to some of Moses' emotional state at this time.

A man in conflict.
A man in struggle.
A man at odds with himself.
A man who is torn and hurting.
A man who has lost sight of himself.
A man who hasn't found contentment.
A man who hasn't come to terms with his identity.
A man who hasn't come to terms with his past or his calling.
A man in between his past and his future.

He stays in Midian for a number of years. In the meantime Pharaoh dies, and the new Pharaoh takes the throne.
The man Moses called brother.
Which leads to the struggle and oppression of his Hebrew brothers increasing, until they cry out to God,

And God heard their cry, because God is the God who hears our cry.

And God remembered His covenant to His people, because God is the God who is faithful.

And God chose to save them, because God is the God who saves.

Moses was out, in the wilderness, in the middle of nowhere. In the middle of his past and his future, tending his sheep.

And God showed up.

Because God meets us where we are.
God shows up in the middle of our nowhere.
God finds us in the wilderness.
God meets us in our brokenness.
God is the God who is with us.

God speaks to Moses about Egypt, and about the cries of the Israelites, the complaints of the Hebrew slaves. And God tells Moses that He is going to send Moses to Pharaoh. His brother. The son of the man who wanted to kill him. The man who is worshipped as a god.

And Moses is to tell Pharaoh to let God's people go.

What could possibly go wrong?

As well as confronting Pharaoh, Moses had to go and tell the Israelites that God was going to save them. Moses had to go to the people who thought he was on the side of Pharaoh. The people who had rejected him. The people who had chased him away. To bring a message from the God they thought had forgotten them. The God they hadn't heard from for generations.

How could this go anything other than beautifully?

God tells Moses that he is the man God has chosen to save the Israelites from slavery. To lead them through the wilderness, and to bring peace and order to them. To establish them as a nation with a land of their own.

All of which leaves Moses convinced that God has got the wrong guy.

Moses will do anything for God, but don't ask him to go back to Egypt. The scene of his greatest pain. The place of his greatest shame and failure. The site of rejection and hurt and brokenness. The location of all the memories that have been haunting him ever since he left.

Anything but that.

Moses argues that he is the wrong guy. He can't speak well. He's past it. He'll get it wrong. It's not who he is. People won't listen to him. Moses is convinced that God has got the wrong man.

But God knows who Moses really is.

Moses has forgotten who he is. Moses has lost sight of his identity. Moses is conflicted. Moses sees the passion that drove him to confront the oppressor of his people as failure and weakness. Moses sees the instinct that caused him to challenge his brothers to be people of peace and unity as stupidity and hot-headedness. Moses sees his experience and skill at guiding sheep through the wilderness as second best and disappointment.

But God sees everything He created Moses to be.

God didn't just call Moses to save one slave from oppression, but a whole nation of them.
God didn't just call Moses to bring peace between two Israelites, but to bring peace and order to a whole nation, establishing them in their own land.
God didn't just call Moses to lead sheep through the wilderness, but to lead a whole nation through the wilderness, to the land God had given them, so that the whole world could be saved.

Now that's a calling.
That's an identity.
That's a story.

Our calling makes sense of who we are. Always.

Rather than calling us to do something entirely other than our gifting or identity, our calling is found in our identity. Our calling makes sense of us. It expresses who we are created to be. And when we allow God to expand our calling within us, to restore us into our God-given identity, then our calling can change the world. It can go beyond our dreams.

But our calling might be found at the scene of our greatest pain. Our calling might mean going back to the things we ran away from. Our calling might be found in the ashes of our greatest failures.

But our calling is always found in our identity.

Our calling is always the thing that makes most sense of who we really are.

Our calling is always at its best when we work it out with God.

Our calling is always at its best when we allow God to do it, and we just go along for the ride.

Our calling is always the path that will lead us to our greatest contentment.

part 3

all

invitation

A number of years ago, I heard a story of a vicar who dressed up as a homeless beggar and camped on the steps of his church. As people arrived they stepped over him, and asked him to move. Nobody invited him in, or gave him a coffee. He asked people for money for food, but nobody gave him anything. He sat in the back of the church, being ignored by everyone, until it was time for the sermon, when he got up, walked to the front, removed his wig and disguise, and preached a sermon on acceptance in the kingdom of God.

So often our church buildings can become quite exclusive places. Wearing the right clothes or looking the right way can be so very important. Smoking or drinking can be frowned upon. As can any number of other factors across the years. There have been times when having different colour skin could be a barrier to acceptance. Being gay, or being a single parent, or being an adulterer, have been cause for rejection. Not wearing a hat, or a tie, or a skirt, or wearing too short a skirt, or jeans has been a barrier.

A reason to exclude.

There have been times when coming from the wrong side of town, or being from the wrong family were a reason to exclude. Tattoos, or piercings, or make up, or haircuts. All sorts of reasons. And so often the Bible has been used to determine the rules which dictate who is allowed in and who is not.

This is what a legalistic framework does to us.
This is how a religious mindset teaches us to think and behave.

When we see the Bible as rules, it divides and excludes. When we see the law as the defining purpose and the sole arbiter, it keeps us rooted at the bottom of the mountain.
We remain distant from God.
It teaches us that we aren't good enough.
It tells us that God is angry with us and wants to punish us.

And the people who define the rules hold all the cards. They have all the power to exclude. We can find ourselves packaging God into a framework which we can use to control and manipulate. Church becomes exclusive. God becomes exclusive. Inaccessible. Scary.

But God's not like that. We have seen that God is a God who loves. A God who desires relationship. We have seen how Paul found that adhering to the law had left him nowhere. A zealous maintaining and defending of the law had left him small, and hardened, and unable to recognise the God he worshipped. It had rendered him lost and distant. It had meant he had become a man who knew about God, but did not know God at all.
He worshipped an unknown God.

The law no longer needs to keep us distant from God. The law no longer needs to tell us that we are unacceptable to God. Jesus came to complete the law. Jesus came to fulfil the law. Jesus came to confront the systems of power and control. Jesus came to confront the religious system that excludes and condemns. Instead, Jesus revealed a God who loves us. A God who is for us. A God who forgives. A God who is in the gutter with the broken, and the lost, and the not good enoughs. A God who isn't angry and violent, but a God of peace. A God of grace.

Grace is the invitation up the mountain.

Not because we have made it, or because we are perfect or holy, but because of who God is, rather than who we are. Grace says we don't have to stay at the bottom of the mountain. We don't have to keep a safe distance. Grace says we can approach God because of who He is and what He has done. We can go up the mountain because of Jesus. Because Jesus confronted the spiritual powers, and the political powers, and the religious powers, and announced a new kingdom where everyone is welcome. Everyone is invited to join in. Everyone can approach God. Everyone can climb the mountain. Because grace is the invitation up the mountain.

Grace says we can go up the mountain, with all our shame, and brokenness, and failure, and disappointment. We can go up the mountain with all our disconnection, and lack, and not enough.

We can go up the mountain as we are. And be KNOWN.

We can know and be known by the unknown God.

What a beautiful image.

What a beautiful idea.

That God, in all His glory, wants to be known.

And as we enter into this relationship with the unfathomable God,
He will take all our shame and brokenness, and disappointment,
and failure, and disconnection, and He will redeem it.

He will lead us into paths of restoration and healing.
Paths of redemption and wholeness.
Paths of confession and forgiveness.
Paths of discovery and wonder.

As we accept this invitation up the mountain,
we accept an invitation to be known by, and to know God.
We accept an invitation into a journey of transformation.
A journey of identity.
As we come to know God and who He is, and what He is like,
we will come to know our true self.
We come to know who we are, and who we are created to be.
And we will begin to look like Him, and show the world around us
something of what God is like.

Now that's an invitation.

fulfilment

Early on in the book of Matthew, Jesus starts his public ministry with a speech to hundreds, or even thousands of people. It's known as the Sermon on the Mount. In it, He talks about the new kingdom He is announcing, and He challenges the established understanding of the scriptures. He also says that He hasn't come to abolish the scriptures, but instead, to fulfil them.

"Don't suppose for a minute that I have come to demolish the Scriptures—either God's Law or the Prophets. I'm not here to demolish but to complete. I am going to put it all together, pull it all together in a vast panorama. God's Law is more real and lasting than the stars in the sky and the ground at your feet. Long after stars burn out and earth wears out, God's Law will be alive and working.
"Trivialize even the smallest item in God's Law and you will only have trivialized yourself. But take it seriously, show the way for others, and you will find honour in the kingdom. Unless you do far better than the Pharisees in the matters of right living, you won't know the first thing about entering the kingdom."

The Message

He says, in a more literal version, that nothing will be removed from the law. That it is complete, and that anyone who does ignore or detract from the law in any way, will be called least in the kingdom. All of which might cause you to wonder why I might be appearing to diminish the law, or suggest that it is irrelevant, or a curse. But those aren't my words, they are Paul's.

We have also seen that Jesus abolished the Temple system, the sacrificial system, and all the laws around cleanliness and food. Jesus seems to abolish the law in so many ways, and yet He says that He didn't come to abolish the law at all, but rather to fulfil it. So, there is some work for us to do if we are going to understand this paradox. It's important that we understand what Jesus is and isn't saying.

We have already seen how removing the legal mindset and having the courage to look at the law in a new way can lead us to discover new life in the scripture.

We have found that when we reject the law as a list of rules we must keep, but instead read it as a revelation of what God is like, that we can enter into relationship with God.

We have seen that when we stop seeing the law as rules which condemn us, but instead as a revelation of who we are created to be, then we are free to go up the mountain and be with God, and the law ceases to be a barrier.

This is what Jesus is talking about in His Sermon on the Mount. If we understand the law as a revelation of who God is, a revelation of who we are called to be, and the reality of all things that we are called to live in, then it makes sense that Jesus is the fulfilment of that law because Jesus is fully God.

Jesus is the fullest revelation of what God is like.
Jesus is the visible image of the invisible God.
Jesus is the embodiment of God.
The Son of God.
The essence of God.
When we look at Jesus, we see what God is like.

But Jesus is also fully human. He is fully human in that He is the fullness of humanity. The revelation of who we are created to be.

People who reflect our creator.
People who are the visible image of the invisible God.
People who create, and love,
People who live lives of blessing and generosity.
People of life, and hope, and beauty.
People who speak life, and forgiveness, and healing.
People who reverse the tide of disconnection and destruction that flows through history.
People who are in deep relationship with God, and who are known fully by God.

Jesus is fully human, and shows us what true humanity looks like. Jesus shows us who God is, and invites us to be participants in His kingdom. People who live in the reality of all things.

Maybe this is what Jesus meant when He said that He had come to fulfil the law.

Maybe He was talking about revealing a God who is the source of all things.
Maybe He was talking about revealing humanity as the image bearers of God to all creation.
Maybe He was talking about revealing the character, and nature, and beauty of God to all creation.
Maybe He was talking about modelling a rhythm of life that teaches us to breathe, and live in harmony with our creator.
Maybe He was talking about revealing a story that is passed on from generation to generation, discovering paths of redemption and wholeness.
Maybe He was talking about revealing a God of life, rather than death. And modelling who we should be. People who speak life, and call out life in creation, rather than people who fight, and kill, and destroy.
Maybe He was talking about revealing a God who is faithful and relational. And modelling how we should be people who love and are faithful, rather than people who lust and betray.
Maybe He was talking about revealing a God of blessing, rather than curses. And modelling how we are created to be people who give, rather than consume. Who are generous, rather than steal.
Who create, rather than destroy.
Maybe He was talking about revealing a God of truth and reality. And modelling how we can be people who live in the reality of all things, rather than people who distort, and lie, and disconnect.
People who discover, and live life as their true selves, rather than feeding and perpetuating their false selves.
Maybe He was talking about revealing a God who is known. And modelling how we can be people who are content. People who know who we are created to be. People who don't have to strive to prove anything, but instead live lives of wholeness, and joy, and peace.

Maybe Jesus fulfilled the law completely.

Which leads us to an intriguing thought.

If Jesus is the full revelation of what God is like, and if He is the fulfilment of the whole law, then what does that say about us?

If Jesus is the revelation of who we are created to be and the revelation of humanity in all its fullness, then is it possible that we could similarly live out that same fullness? Could we, in the same way, fulfil the law? Could we be the revelation of what God is like?

Maybe this is who we were created to be.

As we go up the mountain, with all our baggage, all our stuff, we enter into relationship with God. Not just belief in or knowledge of, but relationship. Intimacy. Knowing each other.
The more we submit to this relationship, the more we submit to the process of healing and restoration and reconnection.The more we become who we were created to be, the more we reveal who God is. The more we enter in to the reality of everything, the more we begin to look like God.

People who find their source of life, and security, and identity, and purpose, and hope from God.
People who reflect that same life and live it out in all creation.
People who act as a conduit of God's blessing.
People who live in rhythm.
People who live out our story, and find paths of wholeness and redemption.
People who bring life.
People who love generously.
People who are faithful.
People who bless, and create, and give.
People who have a grasp on reality.
People who speak truth gently.
People who are content.
People who don't compete and overpower, but instead see the beauty in everyone.
People who pour themselves out and give themselves to see 'the other' become everything they were created to be.
People of hope.

Not people who follow the rules, or insist on the rules.

People who fulfil the law in its fullest sense.

all of me

So, how do we enter this relationship with God?
How do we get to know this unknown God?

The invitation into this relationship is made by Jesus in the gospels.

'Love the lord your God with all your heart, all your soul and
all your strength and all your mind'

NIV

In Deuteronomy, where Jesus takes the original scripture from, it just talks about heart soul and strength, but Jesus seems to add mind. Perhaps He does this in response to the dominance of philosophy in the Greek and Roman cultures which gave great emphasis to the mind, and our understanding.

But what does it mean to love God? And how do we do that with our heart, our soul, our strength and our mind?

Heart is probably the more obvious way we think about loving people. It draws up ideas of passion and intimacy. It has echoes of vulnerability, because love is always risky. Love always puts us in a place where we can be hurt, or rejected, or betrayed, or ignored. Love is when we give ourselves into a situation, or to a person. Love involves sacrifice, and a laying down of self. Preferring 'the other'. All of these are matters of the heart. Strong emotions that stir us, and form us, and shape us. Feelings of connection and desire. Feelings that draw us deeper and closer. Feelings that dominate and consume us. Love of the heart isn't rational, or weak, or measured. It is intense and instinctive. It is passionate. It's something we pursue, and want more of. Love of the heart talks of commitment and faithfulness. It has echoes of covenant and sacrifice. Echoes of joy, and laughter, and tears, and life being lived together. Love of the heart has a lightness and a beauty to it that invites us to go deeper. It invites us to dive in and discover more.

Love of the soul is deeper.

It talks of a profound connection from the core of our being. It's a love that makes sense of us. A love that finds us and forms in us. It's a love that expresses something that we can't find words for.

That's why worship songs can connect with us so much.

Worship is expressed in songs, and liturgy, and language. At its best, it is language that elevates us. Language that transcends the confines of the words and invites us into that space beyond language. That space beyond definitions. And we find God there. The indefinable God. The uncontainable God. The God who will not be restricted to a name.

Language and worship at its best does that. It doesn't restrict, or confine, or define God. It invites us to go beyond, to go deeper into ourselves, and deeper into Him, and connect beyond the language. To explore the ideas and the connections we don't have words for. To explore the aspects of God we can't pin down. And our souls cry out. Not with words but with cries and groans. With pain and with elation. With sorrow and with joy. Deep cries out to deep. And our souls connect and expand, and move in harmony with our creator.

Loving God with our strength is about our actions.

It's about resolve and determination. It talks of pressing in. It talks of courage and energy. And loving God with our strength is about the ways we reflect who God is in our families and communities. All the ways we love and serve others. All the ways we show the world what God is like. In many ways it's a very practical love, but it's also a very determined and focused love. It's a love that always pushes further. A love that commits and works it out. A love that won't give up. A love that perseveres.

Loving God with all our strength is when we push into God to work through our pain and brokenness. It's when we work out our calling and our identity with a determination and a resolve that demands that God meets us in the middle of our struggle. It's when we actively choose life, and healing, and reconnection over and over again. Even when hope has gone. It's a love that is stubborn and resolved. It's a love that refuses to be passive. It's a love that always chooses hope. It's a love that never gives up. A love that always chooses the path of transformation.

It always chooses the path less travelled.

The path of forgiveness and confession and redemption.

Loving God with our mind is about how we think of God, how we think of ourselves, how we think of the world, and how we think.

We are invited in Romans to be transformed by the renewing of our minds. To change how we think. To see the world differently. We are encouraged to allow God to change our perspective of reality, so that our behaviour is changed.

Because the story we live in defines our behaviour.

And so, as we allow God to transform how we see the world, how we know Him and who we know ourselves to be, then we will be changed in the process.

Which means that how we interact with the world will be changed. It means that how we interact and relate with God will be changed, and how we interact with each other will be changed.

Loving God with our mind means allowing the patterns that are forged and formed in our mind to be changed. Where patterns and habits of negativity, or shame, or 'not enough', or addiction used to form, instead we forge patterns of generosity, and forgiveness, and contentment. Patterns of gratitude and creativity. We build constructive life-giving habits and instincts. And we challenge and overcome habits and thought processes that trap us in negative spirals and destructive habits.

Loving God with our mind means allowing ourselves to entertain questions and doubt. It means recognising that we don't have all the answers. We don't have it all figured out yet. Over the years my theology has evolved. There are understandings of scripture, and of God, and of the world around me, that I held when I was a child, but which changed as I grew older. There are theologies and ideas that I held strongly in my teens, which evolved and changed in my twenties. Which evolved, and changed, and developed, and deepened, and shifted through my thirties, and into my forties. How I view God today is different to how I viewed God twenty years ago, or ten years ago, or five years ago. Because relationships are dynamic. We grow together. We evolve. We develop. And as I come into new understandings, encounters, and experiences of God, through love, and intimacy, and worship, and revelation, and prayer, and conversation, so the breadth and depth of my understanding of who God is, has changed and developed and broadened.

As I have encountered God through different people and through different situations, my relationship with God has grown.

As I have wrestled with God and embraced all the questions that swirl through my mind, I have come to know God better and love God more. I have come to enjoy the mystery and the paradox.

As I have seen God work in situations where I didn't expect to find Him, or work through people that I didn't think He would use, or be revealed in, I have grown more comfortable with the idea that God is so infinitely bigger than my understanding. He is so much bigger than I can comprehend or conceive.

As I have studied and wrestled the scriptures, I have seen new aspects to God that I had never seen before. I have discovered new aspects to scripture that I didn't perceive before.
I have discovered new trajectories and themes that weave their way through the Bible.
I have discovered new lenses to see scripture through.
I have found new depths of beauty and harmony.
I have found new melodies and rhythms of life and forgiveness and generosity.
I have found new ways to see and encounter God.

We are called to love God in all these ways.
We are invited, or encouraged, or inspired to love God with all our heart, our soul, our strength and our mind.

This isn't just a God who we get to know about but who remains unknown.
This isn't just a God who we get to believe in but who remains inaccessible.
This isn't just a God who we get to obey, or sing about, or talk about, but who remains distant.

This is a God who wants to love and be loved.

This is a God who wants to know and be known.

This is a God who I can love with every aspect of my being.

A God who I can love with all of me.

all of him

As well as being invited to love God with every aspect of our being, we are also able to love every aspect of God.

We are in relationship with a God in three persons. We are able to connect and engage with a God who is Father, and Son and Spirit. Which means that how we interact and engage with God isn't just about the various aspects of our being. It is also about the various aspects of His being.

We can engage with God the Father, as the God who is our source of life. He is the creator who is our source of creativity. When we engage with God as Father, we engage with the vastness of God. The beauty and wonder of God. The mystery and love of God. In many ways this primarily links with our ability to love God with our minds.

In a similar sense, Jesus seems to link primarily to our ability to love God with our hearts.

Jesus is tangible and relational. He is like us. In the Old Testament God was invisible and distant. We have seen how people would look to a Moses like figure, or a priest, to tell them about the things God had said. They heard stories about the things God had done. God was someone they believed in, but didn't know. But when Jesus comes, now God is tangible. People didn't just have priests to tell them what God said, they could hear it directly. They could see His actions, His miracles, His healings, directly.
Visible. Tangible. Real. Relatable. Lovable.

But God wasn't finished there. Jesus promised that He would leave us with the Holy Spirit.

God in us.

Now we don't just get to hear about God, or even see the things God does, now we get to be the hands and feet. Now we get to speak God's words.

This is a large part of how we love God with our soul. We allow the Spirit of God to flow through us. To work His way through us, and bring His healing, His beauty, His transformation, His power and His love, allowing it to infiltrate every aspect of our being. Every aspect of our soul. Every aspect of our lives.

This way of viewing how we love the different persons of God with the different aspects of ourselves is certainly interesting but by no means exclusive. It is entirely possible to love Jesus with our minds or our souls. To love the Father with our heart or soul, or to love the Spirit with our heart or mind, but there are more obvious connections between the aspects of God and the aspects of us. Which can often mean that we are prone to functioning more naturally with an aspect of ourselves. Which can in turn mean that we are prone to engaging more naturally with an aspect of God, or a particular person of the Trinity.

Let me explain.

I am more naturally intellectual. I find patterns and connections in everything. I spend a lot of time contemplating mysteries. I wrestle with paradoxes, and questions, and ideas. I turn concepts over in my mind, looking at new ways of approaching a question or a problem.

I remember a couple of my parents' evenings at school. In one, my maths teacher explained to my parents that he wasn't sure how to teach me. I would approach maths problems in an unconventional way, and they weren't sure how my mind worked. The problem was that I always got the right answer. Often, I would get the right answer faster than the other students, but when I was asked to show my workings, I couldn't show them, or if I could, it was the wrong process.

Another time, a few years later, my economics teacher described me as esoteric, which I had to look up, but I think he suggested that I worked at a tangent, or approached things in a unique or special way that was outside of the recognised or normal system. I'm still not entirely sure whether he saw it as a good thing.

Because my mind works this way, it would suggest that my more natural way of engaging with God, or loving God, is with my mind.

It seems natural that I would more comfortably engage with the vastness or complexity of God the Father and creator. The beauty and wonder would be more natural to me than the intimacy and relatability of Jesus, or the power and expressiveness of the Spirit.

Others may find the vastness or mystery of God quite intimidating or inaccessible, and be more comfortable with the person of Jesus. A man we can relate to and engage with. Tangible, visible, real, rooted in time and history. Others still, feel far more comfortable with the Holy Spirit. They enjoy and connect with the spirituality of it. The dynamism of it. The power and emotion of it. And so they love to worship, and connect, and flow in the Spirit, seeing it flow through them for the blessing of the people around them. We find the different aspects of God easier or harder to connect with and love. And so, this is a journey that we are invited to explore.

It's too easy to just enjoy what comes most naturally to us. When we do that we miss out on huge aspects of who God is and who we are. Of course, we have our more natural ways of loving, and connecting, but when God says that we should love Him with our heart, and soul, and strength, and mind, it is an invitation to expand ourselves and live in more fullness and wholeness. It is an invitation to stretch ourselves and use the aspects of ourselves we find less natural or obvious.

To engage our minds and embrace the questions and the doubts, if that's more difficult for us.

To engage our hearts and practice vulnerability and intimacy with Jesus, if that is the thing we find most uncomfortable.

To engage our souls and practice obedience and faith, and not being in control, if that's where our greatest fears lie.

We are invited to love and be loved.
We are invited to know and be known.
We are invited to abandon ourselves into the love of God.
All of me.
All of Him.

Known.

all of us

All of this isn't just true for us as individuals. It's also true for us as communities. It's true for us as churches.

In the same way we as individuals often have a favourite way of engaging God, we also have preferences as churches. In the same way we as individuals may connect with a specific aspect of God or person of the Trinity, this can be true of churches too.

Some churches are more focused on teaching. We love to think. We love to wrestle with the challenges of scripture, and the person of God. We love awe and wonder. We love majesty and grandeur. We love the big and the vastness and the beauty of God.

Other churches connect more with Jesus. We love to worship and to evangelise. We love to talk about Jesus, sing about Jesus, and invite others into that same relationship with the God we know so personally.

Other churches love the power and dynamism of the Spirit. We love to see healings and miracles. We love to speak in tongues or have pictures or prophesies for each other. We love to see God in action. Dynamically and powerfully and transformatively.

None of these are in any way wrong.

These are all beautiful ways of engaging with and loving God as a community. But they are one aspect of it.

What if we sought to stretch ourselves as churches?

What if we still pursued our preferred way of engaging God, but at the same time made room to encounter God in new ways. What if those of us who love the awe and wonder of God, and like to wrestle with scripture, made space for the miraculous or the prophetic? What if we stepped out in evangelism more? What if we immersed ourselves in worship more, or wasted time with Jesus?

And what if those of us who love to worship, and evangelise, and focus on the salvation of Jesus, made some space for questions and doubts? Or stepped into more authority of the Spirit, with an expectation of the miraculous and the beautiful?

And what if those of us who thrive in the prophetic and the flow of the Spirit, took more time to sit with Jesus and breathe? Or spent more time serving our community and finding God in the eyes and the lives of the lost and the broken, and the homeless and the hurting, and the addicts and the carers?

And what if all of us, however we love best, and whichever aspect of God we connect with best, saw ourselves as part of something so much bigger?

What if we saw the whole church as our brothers and sisters? Not just the churches and the Christians we agree with, but those who we differ from too? What if we saw ourselves as part of the whole body of Christ, deeply connected with each other and with God?

In the Old Testament we see a model of community which demands that one man goes up the mountain to encounter God and hear God for the whole community, and the role of the community is to do whatever the Moses figure says.

Many of our churches still seem to function in this way. We want our pastor, or minister, or prophet, or worship leader, or vicar, or whoever it is, to go up the mountain and hear God. We want them to convey God's words to us. To inspire us and tell us what God says. We want people to have words or pictures for us so we can know what God wants us to do, or what decisions He wants us to make, or where to go, or who to marry, or whatever it is. I am still asked from time to time what 'we' believe about a particular issue, like I am the spokesman or the decision maker for the whole church. I am sometimes asked to pray for people and let them know what God wants them to do.

We can sometimes seem to hold an aversion to encountering God for ourselves. Tell me what He says. Tell me what to believe. Tell me what to do. But don't make me meet Him for myself. Give me the formula, but don't ask me to submit and step into a relationship with God.

And so, we look to our church leaders, and prophets, and worship leaders. We look to the celebrities, and we believe whatever they say. We sing whatever they write.

And we don't learn to wrestle for ourselves.
We don't learn critical thinking for ourselves.
We don't learn to hear God for ourselves.

But the New Testament isn't supposed to be like that.
The New Testament model of church is supposed to be different.
It's not about a leader or a prophet or a celebrity now.

We aren't called to be churches built around a personality or a pastor, we are called to be churches built around a community. Churches that reflect Christ to the world around them.

Rather than being a people who stay a safe distance from God while the leader goes up the mountain, we are supposed to go up the mountain together. The role of the leader in the New Testament church is to take all the people up the mountain with them. To teach the people to encounter and hear God together. With each other and through each other.
To submit to each other and encourage each other.
To prophesy and pray for each other.
To sit in the presence of God, and carry that blessing to the world around us.

In the church, we go up the mountain together.
We worship together.
We serve together.
We pray together.
We love each other and the other.
We give.
We bless.
We create.
We confess.
We heal.
And we join in the journey of transformation together.
Alongside each other.

Community.

All of us.

all of them

But it doesn't stop with us.

We are not the end of this story.

We are just the next step.

Participants in a much bigger story.

A story we get to tell with every part of us.

A story we get to pass on to our children and to our community.

The blessing doesn't stop with us.
We are blessed to be the blessing.
We are loved so that we can love.
We are created so that we can create.
We are forgiven so we can forgive.
We are included so that we can include.

This story is a story of redemption. This story is a story of the reconciling of all things. And it starts with a man, called Abraham. Abraham is told to leave his land of security and identity and life and purpose. He is told to leave his land of power and strength and violence and war, and to step out into a journey of discovery with God. A journey of identity and redemption. A story of hope and wholeness. This man was told by God that he would have a family, which would bring about the salvation of the world.
The restoration of heaven and earth.
The wholeness of all things.
This family became a tribe, which became slaves in Egypt. God heard the cry of His people, and He saved them, and gave them a land and an identity, and they became a nation. And from that nation came Jesus, who reminded them of who they were created to be.

A blessing to the world.
The visible image of the invisible God.

This good news wasn't intended to be confined to the people of Israel. It was good news for the whole world.

Everyone.

Every tribe. Every nation. Every land. All of them.

It is a trajectory of redemption, and restoration, and love, which is headed somewhere.
This trajectory is arcing towards justice and hope.
This trajectory is arcing towards life and beauty.
This trajectory is arcing towards wholeness.

All things.

All creation.

It doesn't exclude, or condemn, or oppress, or isolate, or diminish, or reject, or dehumanise us.
It invites us into paths of wholeness.
It invites us to be everything we were created to be.
It invites us to include, and love, and prefer, and serve, and give.
It invites us to reconnect in every way we can. To reconnect with God in every way we can, with every part of our being.

To reconnect within ourselves, and rediscover who we were created to be. To choose paths of redemption and wholeness.
Paths of confession and forgiveness.
Paths of life and paths of blessing.

To reconnect with each other, learning to love, and include, and prefer, and forgive.
Learning to see God in each other, and 'the other'.
Learning to agree with God about each person in His creation.
Recognising them as beautiful image-bearers of the creator.
People with limitless potential and gifting.
People of immense worth.

And to reconnect with creation. In every way we can.
Learning to see all the ways in which we are connected with every aspect of creation. Learning to recognise the beauty of it all.
Learning to see the interconnectedness of everything.

Learning to live in harmony with creation. Learning to live lives that bless the world and creation. Learning to be givers rather than consumers.

We are invited to reconnect in every way we can, so that the world around us can be reconnected, restored and renewed in every way it can.

This is the kingdom that Jesus announced.
This is the kingdom that we are invited into.
This is the kingdom we are participants in.

This is the story we are part of.
This is the story we get to join in.
All of us.
This is a story that doesn't divide or exclude.
It doesn't set man against woman, or family against family, or tribe against tribe, or nation against nation.
This is a story that doesn't set us at odds with each other, or in competition with each other.

This story of forgiveness and hope is a story for everyone.

This story of confession and restoration is a story for everyone.

This story of judgement and wholeness is a story for everyone.

This story of love and relationship is a story for everyone.

This story of reconnection and rehumanisation is a story for everyone.

Everyone.

All of us.

All of them.

E V E R Y O N E

The End

About the Author

Adam Dyer has been leader of Yeovil Community Church since 2008.

As a church, and as part of the wider church in Yeovil, YCC are deeply engaged with the community, running a vast range of projects and initiatives to support all aspects of the community. This includes pioneering the 4Family programme which works closely with the full array of local agencies to support the families and individuals most in need of support in the community. This programme is now being replicated in towns, cities and churches across the country.

Adam is a communicator of hope who brings fresh and exciting perspectives to scripture, faith and church. His engaging style and challenging insights inspire people to discover new aspects of God, and to live out their faith in an authentic way.

He is also South West Regional Advisor for the Cinnamon Network, supporting churches all over the region to engage with their civic leaders and their whole community.

Adam is an innovator of church and community, who inspires new ways of modelling church that enables everyone to join in. Adam supports churches with developing vision and values, as well as strategies to engage the whole church in community transformation.

If you would like to to book Adam to speak at your church, or conference, or to support your leadership team as a consultant, please contact

adam.dyer@yeovilcommunitychurch.co.uk

you can follow Adam on Twitter @adamycc

or you can listen to the latest sermons at

www.yeovilcommunitychurch.co.uk